THE GALVESTON DIET COOKBOOK FOR BEGINNERS 2025

Super Easy Healthy & Delicious Recipes to Aid in Weight Loss, Anti-inflammation and Help Hormonal Imbalance | Includes 30-Day Meal Plan

Walter Rivers

Copyright © 2024 by Walter Rivers

All rights reserved. No part of this publication may be reproduced, stored in a retrieval system, or transmitted in any form or by any means, electronic, mechanical, photocopying, recording, or otherwise, without the prior written permission of the publisher or author, except for brief quotations for review purposes.

This publication is intended for informational purposes only and does not constitute legal, investment, accounting, or other professional advice. While every effort has been made to ensure the accuracy of the information contained herein, the author and publisher disclaim any liability for errors or omissions.

The information presented in this book is not a substitute for professional advice. Readers should consult with appropriate professionals before making any decisions based on the information in this book. The author and publisher shall not be liable for any damages, including but not limited to special, incidental, consequential, or other damages, arising from the use or reliance on any information contained in this book

CONTENTS

INTRODUCTION 1
   Understanding the Basics 2
   Shopping Tips 2
   Tips for Long-Term Success 4

CHAPTER 1: BREAKFAST 6
   Avocado & Spinach Breakfast Smoothie 6
   Keto Chia Seed Pudding with Fresh Berries 7
   Egg White & Veggie Frittata 8
   Almond Flour Pancakes with Sugar-Free Syrup 9
   Smoked Salmon & Avocado Breakfast Bowl 10
   Coconut Yogurt Parfait with Chopped Nuts 11
   Cauliflower Hash Browns with Poached Eggs 12
   Spicy Egg Muffins with Bell Peppers 13
   Zucchini Noodles Breakfast Bowl with Pesto 14
   Cinnamon Flaxseed Porridge 15
   Low-Carb Breakfast Burrito with Turkey Sausage 16
   Keto Avocado Toast on Almond Flour Bread 17
   Berry & Coconut Smoothie Bowl 18
   Sautéed Mushrooms & Spinach Omelet 19
   Bacon-Wrapped Asparagus with Soft-Boiled Eggs 20
   Matcha Coconut Latte 21
   Blueberry-Almond Protein Smoothie 22

CHAPTER 2: LIGHT BITES & SNACKS 23
   Cucumber & Smoked Salmon Roll-Ups 23
   Keto-Friendly Cheese Crisps 24
   Zucchini Chips with Herb Dip 25
   Spicy Almond Butter Energy Balls 26
   Roasted Garlic & Parmesan Kale Chips 27
   Stuffed Mini Bell Peppers with Cream Cheese 28
   Crispy Avocado Fries 29
   Mini Caprese Skewers with Balsamic Glaze 30
   Cauliflower Hummus with Veggie Sticks 31
   Deviled Eggs with Smoked Paprika 32
   Baked Buffalo Cauliflower Bites 33
   Almond Butter and Celery Sticks 34

Keto-Friendly Trail Mix with Nuts & Seeds 35

Garlic & Herb Roasted Pumpkin Seeds 36

Mini Cucumber Sandwiches with Turkey & Avocado 37

Spicy Tuna Salad Lettuce Wraps 38

Frozen Coconut Berry Bites 39

CHAPTER 3: LUNCH 40

Grilled Chicken & Avocado Salad with Lime Vinaigrette 40

Creamy Broccoli & Cheddar Soup 41

Keto Taco Salad with Ground Turkey 42

Spinach & Feta Stuffed Portobello Mushrooms 43

Asian-Inspired Shrimp & Cabbage Stir-Fry 44

Cauliflower Fried "Rice" with Beef 45

Lemon-Dill Salmon Lettuce Wraps 46

Greek Chicken Salad with Cucumber & Olives 47

Zucchini Noodle Alfredo with Grilled Chicken 48

Low-Carb BLT Wraps 49

Garlic & Herb Roasted Veggie Bowl 50

Curried Cauliflower Soup with Coconut Milk 51

Italian Meatball Zoodle Soup 52

Balsamic Chicken & Roasted Veggie Sheet Pan Meal 53

Tuna & Egg Salad on Butter Lettuce 54

Cajun Shrimp & Avocado Salad 55

CHAPTER 4: DINNER 56

Garlic Butter Baked Salmon with Asparagus 56

Zesty Lemon-Herb Chicken Thighs 57

Beef & Veggie Stir-Fry with Coconut Aminos 58

Sheet Pan Shrimp Fajitas 59

Spaghetti Squash with Pesto & Grilled Chicken 60

Cauliflower Crust Margherita Pizza 61

Keto-Friendly Lasagna with Zucchini Noodles 62

Seared Ahi Tuna with Ginger-Cucumber Slaw 63

Rosemary-Garlic Pork Tenderloin 64

Miso Cod with Bok Choy 65

Chicken & Mushroom Creamy Cauliflower Rice 66

Greek-Inspired Lamb Burgers with Tzatziki Sauce 67

Slow-Cooked Beef Stew with Root Vegetables 68

Stuffed Bell Peppers with Ground Turkey & Veggies 69

Roasted Lemon-Garlic Brussels Sprouts & Sausage 70

Thai-Inspired Coconut Curry Chicken 71

Herbed Butter Roasted Whole Chicken 72

CHAPTER 5: VEGGIES & SIDES 73

Garlic Parmesan Roasted Broccoli 73

Spicy Cauliflower Rice Pilaf 73

Balsamic Glazed Brussels Sprouts with Pecans 74

Zoodles with Sun-Dried Tomato & Olive Tapenade 74

Grilled Asparagus with Lemon Zest 75

Roasted Rainbow Carrots with Thyme 75

Crispy Baked Kale with Sea Salt 76

Cheesy Cauliflower Mash 76

Spicy Sautéed Spinach with Garlic 77

Buttery Cabbage Steaks 77

Cauliflower "Mac & Cheese" 78

Roasted Radishes with Rosemary 78

Creamy Avocado & Cucumber Salad 79

Sautéed Mushrooms with Fresh Herbs 79

Baked Zucchini Fries 80

Garlic Lemon Green Beans 80

Sweet & Spicy Roasted Butternut Squash 81

CHAPTER 6: DESSERTS & SWEET TREATS 82

Keto Chocolate Mousse with Coconut Cream 82

Almond Flour Shortbread Cookies 83

Baked Cinnamon Apples with Walnuts 84

No-Bake Lemon Cheesecake Cups 85

Dark Chocolate & Sea Salt Fat Bombs 86

Raspberry Chia Seed Pudding 87

Coconut Almond Bliss Balls 88

Keto-Friendly Pumpkin Spice Muffins 89

Blueberry Crumble with Almond Topping 90

Vanilla Bean Coconut Ice Cream 91

Chocolate Avocado Pudding 92

Low-Carb Peanut Butter Bars 93

Strawberry Coconut Popsicles 94

Mini Berry Cheesecakes 95

Baked Pears with Cinnamon and Almonds 96

 Keto-Friendly Chocolate Chip Blondies 97

 Matcha Coconut Fudge 98

CHAPTER 7: BEVERAGES & SMOOTHIES 99

 Green Detox Smoothie with Spinach & Pineapple 99

 Golden Turmeric Latte 99

 Cucumber Mint Infused Water 100

 Almond Butter & Banana Protein Shake 100

 Keto Iced Matcha Latte 101

 Berry-Mint Lemonade 101

 Avocado Green Smoothie 102

 Anti-Inflammatory Ginger Tea 102

 Strawberry & Basil Infused Sparkling Water 103

 Spiced Chai Coconut Milk Latte 103

 Low-Carb Chocolate Peanut Butter Smoothie 104

 Citrus & Mint Green Tea Cooler 104

 Keto Pumpkin Spice Coffee 105

 Blueberry-Cucumber Hydration Smoothie 105

 Ginger & Lemon Detox Water 106

 Almond Milk Hot Chocolate 106

 Mango-Turmeric Smoothie 107

30-DAY MEAL PLAN 108

MEASUREMENT CONVERSION TABLE 110

CONCLUSION 111

RECIPES INDEX 112

INTRODUCTION

Welcome to The Galveston Diet Cookbook for Newbies. This cookbook aims to make your experience with the Galveston Diet straightforward, fun, and tasty. You're in the right spot if you want to boost your metabolic health, balance your hormones, or simply live a healthier life.

The Galveston Diet emphasizes an anti-inflammatory method, highlighting healthy fats, lean proteins, and low-carb vegetables. This eating style honors your body's needs, helping you lower inflammation, boost energy, and feel great daily. This cookbook is designed for beginners, featuring a range of recipes that are delightfully simple to make and include common ingredients, ensuring you can cook with confidence.

As a chef, I've spent many years in kitchens trying out different flavors and techniques. My love for cooking became more personal when I dealt with weight gain and fatigue in my 40s. Even though I'm skilled at making delicious meals, I struggled to find a balance between my passion for food and the needs of my changing body. That's when I found out about the Galveston Diet. I understand the challenges you may face, and I'm here to guide you through them.

This diet taught me how to take care of myself while keeping my energy up and enjoying tasty food. The recipes I've included are not only designed for a specific dietary plan; they are meals I prepare for my family, bringing joy to our table. I'm excited to share these with you, and I hope each recipe inspires you to be creative in your kitchen.

Put on your apron, and let's begin this tasty adventure together! Whether you're new to the Galveston Diet or seeking fresh ideas, I'm here to help you enjoy it in your daily routine.

Understanding the Basics

The Galveston Diet focuses on three main ideas: lowering inflammation, choosing whole, nutrient-rich foods, and incorporating intermittent fasting. All of these elements come together to support you in achieving your health goals, whether you want to manage your weight, balance your hormones, or enhance your overall well-being. This approach is effective for a few key reasons:

1. Anti-Inflammatory Eating

The Galveston Diet focuses on lowering chronic inflammation, which can lead to weight gain, tiredness, and different health issues. This diet includes anti-inflammatory foods such as leafy greens, fatty fish, avocados, nuts, and seeds. It also reduces refined sugars, processed foods, and trans fats, which may cause inflammation. When you pick whole foods that are rich in nutrients, you're giving your body the support it needs to flourish.

2. Healthy Fats and Lean Proteins

The Galveston Diet stands out from many traditional diets by highlighting the significance of healthy fats and proteins. Foods such as olive oil, nuts, salmon, and lean meats are filling and help maintain hormone balance, keeping you satisfied for a longer time. Healthy fats are essential for your brain and help your body take in important vitamins. Lean proteins help build muscles and boost metabolism, making you feel full without adding extra carbs.

3. Intermittent Fasting

Intermittent fasting is an important part of the Galveston Diet. It promotes cycles of eating and fasting to help with metabolism and energy management. One popular method is the 16:8 approach, which involves eating within an 8-hour window and fasting for 16 hours. This can assist in managing blood sugar levels, support fat burning, and enhance digestion. Aligning your meals with your body's natural rhythms can boost your energy and focus during the day.

Grasping these fundamentals is the initial move to making the Galveston Diet effective. By taking the right steps, you'll quickly notice how these little adjustments can make a big difference in your daily feelings.

Shopping Tips

Starting on the Galveston Diet can be made easier with some strategic shopping. A well-stocked kitchen filled with the right ingredients will set you up for success, making it easier to prepare nourishing meals and stick to your goals. Here are some shopping tips to help you get started:

1. Make a List and Stick to It

Before heading to the grocery store, plan your weekly meals and make a shopping list based on those recipes. This will help you avoid impulse buys, save money, and ensure you have everything you need for the week. Focus on Galveston Diet staples like fresh vegetables, lean proteins, and healthy fats.

2. Shop the Perimeter of the Store

You'll find most of the fresh, whole foods you need for the Galveston Diet along the edges of the store—like fruits, vegetables, meats, seafood, and dairy products. Avoid the inner aisles, as they usually have processed and packaged foods. Stock up on a mix of fresh vegetables, leafy greens, and seasonal fruits to make your meals colorful and exciting.

3. Choose Organic When Possible

Buying organic isn't required, but selecting organic fruits, vegetables, and meats can help you steer clear of pesticides and hormones. When shopping, choose organic for the "Dirty Dozen"—fruits and vegetables such as strawberries, spinach, and apples that often have pesticide residues. Conventional produce is still a healthy option and is usually easier on the wallet for other items.

4. Stock Up on Pantry Essentials

A well-stocked pantry is essential for following the Galveston Diet. Have essentials such as extra-virgin olive oil, avocado oil, nuts, seeds, canned salmon, coconut milk, and low-carb flours (like almond flour) ready to use. These items are flexible and can enhance the flavor and texture of a variety of recipes.

5. Buy in Bulk for Healthy Fats and Proteins

Buying nuts, seeds, lean meats, and fish in bulk can help you save money and keep protein-rich options available at home. If you have room in your freezer, think about buying lean cuts of meat or seafood in bulk and freezing them for future meals. This makes preparing meals easier and helps you steer clear of those last-minute store runs.

6. Read Labels Carefully

Always check the ingredient labels when purchasing packaged foods such as salad dressings, sauces, or snacks. Be aware of hidden sugars, refined oils, and additives that don't fit with the Galveston Diet. Choose products that have straightforward ingredients and no extra sugars. This simple habit can greatly help in keeping your meals on track.

7. Explore Local Farmers' Markets

Local farmers' markets are a wonderful way to discover fresh, seasonal fruits and vegetables while supporting local farmers. You'll often come across organic fruits and vegetables, grass-fed meats, and other top-notch ingredients that fit nicely with the diet. Additionally, trying out new seasonal vegetables or fruits can bring some excitement to your meals.

8. Don't Forget Meal Prep Containers

When you go shopping, consider getting some BPA-free glass storage containers or meal prep containers. These will help you store leftovers, prepare meals in batches, and keep your fridge tidy. Preparing meals in advance can help you save time during hectic weeks and keep you focused on your goals.

With these shopping tips, you'll have everything you need to create tasty, Galveston Diet-friendly meals at home. With a bit of planning, your diet journey can be smooth and enjoyable!

Tips for Long-Term Success

Choosing the Galveston Diet means more than just altering your meals—it's about building a way of life that promotes your health and happiness for the future. Starting a new diet can be exciting, but keeping that energy going takes careful planning. Check out these tips for reaching long-term success on the Galveston Diet:

1. Focus on Progress, Not Perfection

It's simple to focus on sticking to the diet flawlessly, but remember that making progress matters more than being perfect. If you have a day when you don't stick to the plan, be kind to yourself. Just refocus and get back on track with your next meal. Seeing setbacks as chances to learn instead of failures can keep you motivated.

2. Make Meal Prep a Habit

Making meal prep a weekly habit is one of the keys to long-term success. Taking time to plan and prepare your meals for the week can help you resist the urge to make unhealthy choices when things get hectic. Prepare proteins in batches, cut up vegetables, and divide snacks ahead of time. With some planning, you'll always have meals that fit the Galveston Diet ready to enjoy.

3. Stay Hydrated

Proper hydration is essential for overall health and can support weight loss and metabolism. Aim to drink plenty of water throughout the day, and consider adding in herbal teas or infused water with lemon, mint, or cucumber for added flavor. Staying hydrated also helps to curb unnecessary snacking, as thirst is often mistaken for hunger.

4. Track Your Progress

Tracking your progress can be a powerful motivator. Consider keeping a journal where you note your meals, how you're feeling, and any changes you notice in your body and energy levels. This can help you identify what works best for you and make adjustments as needed. Additionally, seeing your progress over time can keep you inspired and remind you why you started this journey.

5. Build a Support System

Having a support system can make a significant difference in maintaining long-term success. Connect with friends, family, or online communities who are also following the Galveston Diet. Sharing experiences, recipes, and encouragement can keep you motivated and help you feel more connected. If possible, find a buddy to join you on your journey, so you can hold each other accountable.

6. Focus on Whole Foods, Not Just the Scale

While weight loss might be a primary goal, focusing on the broader benefits of the Galveston Diet—such as increased energy, improved digestion, and better mood—can help you stay committed over time. Celebrate non-scale victories like feeling more energetic or noticing clearer skin. These positive changes will remind you that the diet is about improving your overall health, not just achieving a certain number on the scale.

7. Adjust the Plan to Fit Your Lifestyle

It's important to remember that the Galveston Diet is not a one-size-fits-all solution. Feel free to adjust your eating schedule, meal plans, and fasting windows to fit your lifestyle and preferences. By making the diet work for you, rather than forcing yourself into a rigid structure, you'll find it easier to stick with it in the long run.

8. Practice Mindful Eating

Mindful eating involves paying attention to your hunger cues, eating slowly, and genuinely savoring your meals. This approach can prevent overeating and help you develop a healthier relationship with food. Sit down at the table, put away distractions, and take the time to enjoy each bite. You'll find that you feel more satisfied with less food when you focus on eating mindfully.

9. Keep Trying New Recipes

Mixing things up is important for staying engaged and preventing exhaustion. Try out new recipes, play around with various flavors, and be imaginative in the kitchen. This cookbook is only the start—adding new ideas to your menu will make every meal something to look forward to.

10. Be Patient with Yourself

Finally, give yourself some time to adjust to this new way of eating. Making lasting changes takes time, and your body might need several weeks or even months to fully adapt. Celebrate the little achievements and keep in mind that every step you take towards better health is a positive move forward.

By adding these tips to your routine, you'll be on track to make the Galveston Diet a lasting part of your life. If you stay dedicated, flexible, and positive, you can achieve long-term success and enjoy the rewards of a healthy lifestyle for many years.

CHAPTER 1: BREAKFAST

Avocado & Spinach Breakfast Smoothie

Time to Prepare: 5 minutes
Cook Time: 0 minutes
Servings: 2

List of Ingredients:

- 1 ripe avocado, peeled and pitted
- 2 cups of fresh spinach
- 1 cup of unsweetened almond milk
- 1/2 cup of coconut water (no added sugars)
- 1/2 cup of frozen mixed berries (strawberries, blueberries, raspberries)
- 1 tablespoon chia seeds
- 1 tablespoon almond butter
- 1 teaspoon of fresh lemon juice
- Ice cubes (optional)

Instructions:

1. Combine all ingredients in a blender.
2. Blend until smooth and creamy. Add ice cubes if a thicker consistency is desired.
3. Taste and adjust sweetness with a few drops of stevia or monk fruit if needed.
4. Pour into two glasses and enjoy immediately.

Nutritional Information (Per Serving):

- Total calories: 240
- Protein: 6g
- Fiber content: 9g
- Carbs: 14g
- Fats: 18g

Keto Chia Seed Pudding with Fresh Berries

Time to Prepare: 5 minutes (plus 4 hours chilling time)
Cook Time: 0 minutes
Servings: 2

List of Ingredients:

- 1/4 cup of chia seeds
- 1 1/2 cups of unsweetened almond milk
- 1 teaspoon of vanilla extract
- 1 tablespoon unsweetened shredded coconut
- 1-2 teaspoons of monk fruit sweetener (to taste)
- 1/2 cup of mixed fresh berries (blueberries, raspberries, strawberries)

Instructions:

1. In a medium bowl, whisk together chia seeds, almond milk, vanilla extract, shredded coconut, and monk fruit sweetener until well mixed.
2. Cover the bowl and refrigerate for at least 4 hours or overnight until the mixture thickens to a pudding-like consistency.
3. Stir the pudding before serving, and divide into two portions.
4. Top each serving with fresh mixed berries and enjoy.

Nutritional Information (Per Serving):

- Total calories: 180
- Protein: 5g
- Fiber content: 10g
- Carbs: 12g
- Fats: 12g

Egg White & Veggie Frittata

Time to Prepare: 10 minutes
Cook Time: 15 minutes
Servings: 4

List of Ingredients:

- 2 cups of egg whites
- 1 cup of baby spinach, chopped
- 1/2 cup of bell pepper, diced (red, yellow, or green)
- 1/2 cup of cherry tomatoes, halved
- 1/4 cup of onion, finely chopped
- 1/4 cup of unsweetened almond milk
- 1 tablespoon avocado oil
- Salt and pepper to taste

Instructions:

1. Preheat oven to 375°F (190°C).
2. Heat avocado oil in a large oven-safe skillet over medium heat. Add onion and bell pepper, and sauté until softened, about 3-4 minutes.
3. Add spinach and cherry tomatoes to the skillet, and cook for another 2 minutes until the spinach wilts.
4. In a separate bowl, whisk together egg whites, almond milk, salt, and pepper. Pour the mixture over the veggies in the skillet.
5. Cook on the stovetop for 2-3 minutes until the edges start to set, then transfer the skillet to the preheated oven.
6. Bake for 10 minutes or until the frittata is set in the center and lightly golden.
7. Slice into 4 pieces and serve warm.

Nutritional Information (Per Serving):

- Total calories: 100
- Protein: 12g
- Fiber content: 2g
- Carbs: 4g
- Fats: 4g

Almond Flour Pancakes with Sugar-Free Syrup

Time to Prepare: 5 minutes
Cook Time: 10 minutes
Servings: 4

List of Ingredients:

- 1 cup of almond flour
- 2 large eggs
- 1/4 cup of unsweetened almond milk
- 1 teaspoon of vanilla extract
- 1 teaspoon of baking powder
- 1 tablespoon monk fruit sweetener
- 1 tablespoon avocado oil (for cooking)
- Sugar-free syrup, for serving

Instructions:

1. In a bowl, whisk together almond flour, eggs, almond milk, vanilla extract, baking powder, and monk fruit sweetener until smooth.
2. Heat a non-stick skillet over medium heat and add a little avocado oil.
3. Pour 1/4 cup of the batter onto the skillet for each pancake. Cook until bubbles form on the surface, about 2-3 minutes, then flip and cook for another 1-2 minutes until golden brown.
4. Repeat with the remaining batter, adding more oil if needed.
5. Serve pancakes warm with sugar-free syrup.

Nutritional Information (Per Serving):

- Total calories: 180
- Protein: 7g
- Fiber content: 3g
- Carbs: 5g
- Fats: 14g

Smoked Salmon & Avocado Breakfast Bowl

Time to Prepare: 10 minutes
Cook Time: 0 minutes
Servings: 2

List of Ingredients:

- 4 ounces smoked salmon, sliced
- 1 ripe avocado, sliced
- 2 cups of mixed greens (spinach, arugula, or lettuce)
- 1/2 cup of cucumber, sliced
- 1/4 cup of red onion, thinly sliced
- 2 tablespoons capers
- 1 tablespoon extra-virgin olive oil
- 1 tablespoon fresh lemon juice
- Salt and pepper to taste

Instructions:

1. Divide mixed greens between two bowls.
2. Arrange smoked salmon, avocado slices, cucumber, and red onion on top of the greens.
3. Sprinkle capers over each bowl.
4. Drizzle with olive oil and fresh lemon juice, and season with salt and pepper to taste.
5. Serve immediately.

Nutritional Information (Per Serving):

- Total calories: 320
- Protein: 16g
- Fiber content: 7g
- Carbs: 10g
- Fats: 25g

Coconut Yogurt Parfait with Chopped Nuts

Time to Prepare: 5 minutes
Cook Time: 0 minutes
Servings: 2

List of Ingredients:

- 1 cup of unsweetened coconut yogurt
- 1/2 cup of mixed berries (blueberries, raspberries, strawberries)
- 1/4 cup of mixed chopped nuts (almonds, walnuts, pecans)
- 1 tablespoon unsweetened shredded coconut
- 1 teaspoon of chia seeds
- 1-2 teaspoons of monk fruit sweetener (to taste)

Instructions:

1. In each serving glass, layer 1/2 cup of coconut yogurt.
2. Top with a layer of mixed berries.
3. Sprinkle chopped nuts, shredded coconut, and chia seeds over the berries.
4. Add a sprinkle of monk fruit sweetener if desired.
5. Repeat the layers and serve immediately.

Nutritional Information (Per Serving):

- Total calories: 220
- Protein: 5g
- Fiber content: 6g
- Carbs: 12g
- Fats: 18g

Cauliflower Hash Browns with Poached Eggs

Time to Prepare: 10 minutes
Cook Time: 15 minutes
Servings: 2

List of Ingredients:

- 2 cups of grated cauliflower
- 1/4 cup of almond flour
- 1 egg
- 1/4 teaspoon of garlic powder
- Salt and pepper to taste
- 1 tablespoon avocado oil (for cooking)
- 4 large eggs (for poaching)
- 1 tablespoon white vinegar (for poaching water)

Instructions:

1. In a bowl, combine grated cauliflower, almond flour, 1 egg, garlic powder, salt, and pepper. Mix until well mixed.
2. Heat avocado oil in a non-stick skillet over medium heat. Form the cauliflower mixture into small patties and cook for 3-4 minutes on each side until golden brown and crispy.
3. In a separate pot, bring water to a gentle simmer and add white vinegar.
4. Crack eggs one at a time into a small bowl and gently slide each egg into the simmering water. Poach for 3-4 minutes until whites are set but yolks remain runny.
5. Serve each poached egg over the crispy cauliflower hash browns.

Nutritional Information (Per Serving):

- Total calories: 250
- Protein: 14g
- Fiber content: 4g
- Carbs: 8g
- Fats: 18g

Spicy Egg Muffins with Bell Peppers

Time to Prepare: 10 minutes
Cook Time: 20 minutes
Servings: 4

List of Ingredients:

- 8 large eggs
- 1/2 cup of diced bell peppers (red, yellow, or green)
- 1/4 cup of diced onion
- 1/2 teaspoon of chili flakes
- 1/2 teaspoon of smoked paprika
- Salt and pepper to taste
- 1 tablespoon avocado oil (for greasing muffin tin)

Instructions:

1. Preheat oven to 350°F (175°C) and grease a muffin tin with avocado oil.
2. In a large bowl, whisk together eggs, chili flakes, smoked paprika, salt, and pepper.
3. Stir in the diced bell peppers and onion until evenly mixed.
4. Pour the egg mixture evenly into the greased muffin tin cups.
5. Bake for 18-20 minutes or until the egg muffins are set and slightly golden on top.
6. Let cool for a few minutes before removing from the tin and serving.

Nutritional Information (Per Serving):

- Total calories: 140
- Protein: 11g
- Fiber content: 1g
- Carbs: 3g
- Fats: 10g

Zucchini Noodles Breakfast Bowl with Pesto

Time to Prepare: 10 minutes
Cook Time: 5 minutes
Servings: 2

List of Ingredients:

- 2 medium zucchinis, spiralized
- 1/4 cup of homemade or store-bought pesto (sugar-free)
- 2 large eggs
- 1 tablespoon avocado oil
- Salt and pepper to taste
- 1 tablespoon grated Parmesan cheese (optional)
- Cherry tomatoes, halved (for garnish)

Instructions:

1. Heat avocado oil in a skillet over medium heat. Add spiralized zucchini noodles and sauté for 2-3 minutes until slightly tender. Season with salt and pepper.
2. In a separate pan, cook the eggs to your liking (poached, fried, or scrambled).
3. Remove the skillet from heat and stir in the pesto until the zucchini noodles are well coated.
4. Divide the zucchini noodles between two bowls and top each with a cooked egg.
5. Garnish with cherry tomatoes and sprinkle with grated Parmesan cheese if desired. Serve immediately.

Nutritional Information (Per Serving):

- Total calories: 220
- Protein: 10g
- Fiber content: 4g
- Carbs: 8g
- Fats: 18g

Cinnamon Flaxseed Porridge

Time to Prepare: 5 minutes
Cook Time: 10 minutes
Servings: 2

List of Ingredients:

- 1/2 cup of ground flaxseeds
- 1 cup of unsweetened almond milk
- 1 tablespoon chia seeds
- 1 teaspoon of cinnamon
- 1 tablespoon monk fruit sweetener (or to taste)
- 1/4 teaspoon of vanilla extract
- Toppings: sliced almonds, berries, or unsweetened coconut flakes

Instructions:

1. In a medium saucepan, combine ground flaxseeds, almond milk, chia seeds, cinnamon, monk fruit sweetener, and vanilla extract.
2. Cook over medium heat, stirring frequently, for about 5-7 minutes until the mixture thickens to a porridge-like consistency.
3. Remove from heat and let sit for a minute to thicken further.
4. Divide the porridge into two bowls and add desired toppings such as sliced almonds, berries, or unsweetened coconut flakes. Serve warm.

Nutritional Information (Per Serving):

- Total calories: 210
- Protein: 7g
- Fiber content: 12g
- Carbs: 8g
- Fats: 16g

Low-Carb Breakfast Burrito with Turkey Sausage

Time to Prepare: 10 minutes
Cook Time: 15 minutes
Servings: 2

List of Ingredients:

- 4 large eggs
- 4 ounces turkey sausage, cooked and crumbled
- 1/2 cup of bell peppers, diced
- 1/4 cup of onion, diced
- 1/2 avocado, sliced
- 1 tablespoon avocado oil (for cooking)
- 1 teaspoon of cumin
- Salt and pepper to taste
- 2 large lettuce leaves (for wrapping)
- Fresh salsa (optional, for serving)

Instructions:

1. In a skillet, heat avocado oil over medium heat. Add diced onion and bell peppers, cooking until softened, about 3-4 minutes.
2. Add the crumbled turkey sausage to the skillet and cook for an additional 2-3 minutes until heated through.
3. In a bowl, whisk together eggs, cumin, salt, and pepper. Pour the egg mixture into the skillet and scramble until fully cooked, about 3-4 minutes.
4. Lay out the lettuce leaves and spoon the turkey sausage and egg mixture into the center of each leaf.
5. Top with avocado slices and drizzle with fresh salsa if desired. Wrap the lettuce around the filling and serve.

Nutritional Information (Per Serving):

- Total calories: 290
- Protein: 24g
- Fiber content: 6g
- Carbs: 7g
- Fats: 20g

Keto Avocado Toast on Almond Flour Bread

Time to Prepare: 10 minutes
Cook Time: 20 minutes
Servings: 2

List of Ingredients:

- 2 slices almond flour bread (store-bought or homemade)
- 1 ripe avocado, mashed
- 1 tablespoon lemon juice
- 1/4 teaspoon of garlic powder
- Salt and pepper to taste
- 1/4 teaspoon of red pepper flakes (optional)
- 2 tablespoons sliced cherry tomatoes (for garnish)
- Fresh herbs (such as cilantro or parsley, for garnish)

Instructions:

1. Preheat the oven to 350°F (175°C). If using homemade almond flour bread, bake it according to your recipe instructions until golden brown.
2. In a bowl, combine the mashed avocado, lemon juice, garlic powder, salt, and pepper. Mix until smooth.
3. Toast the almond flour bread slices in the oven or a toaster until crispy, about 5-7 minutes.
4. Spread the avocado mixture evenly over each slice of toasted bread.
5. Garnish with sliced cherry tomatoes, red pepper flakes, and fresh herbs. Serve immediately.

Nutritional Information (Per Serving):

- Total calories: 320
- Protein: 8g
- Fiber content: 10g
- Carbs: 6g
- Fats: 28g

Berry & Coconut Smoothie Bowl

Time to Prepare: 5 minutes
Cook Time: 0 minutes
Servings: 2

List of Ingredients:

- 1 cup of unsweetened coconut yogurt
- 1 cup of frozen mixed berries (blueberries, strawberries, raspberries)
- 1/2 cup of unsweetened almond milk
- 1 tablespoon chia seeds
- 1 tablespoon unsweetened shredded coconut
- 1 tablespoon monk fruit sweetener (optional, to taste)
- Toppings: fresh berries, sliced almonds, and coconut flakes

Instructions:

1. In a blender, combine coconut yogurt, frozen mixed berries, almond milk, chia seeds, shredded coconut, and monk fruit sweetener. Blend until smooth and creamy.
2. Pour the smoothie mixture into two bowls.
3. Top with fresh berries, sliced almonds, and additional coconut flakes as desired.
4. Serve immediately with a spoon.

Nutritional Information (Per Serving):

- Total calories: 230
- Protein: 6g
- Fiber content: 8g
- Carbs: 12g
- Fats: 18g

Sautéed Mushrooms & Spinach Omelet

Time to Prepare: 5 minutes
Cook Time: 10 minutes
Servings: 2

List of Ingredients:

- 4 large eggs
- 1 cup of fresh spinach, chopped
- 1 cup of mushrooms, sliced (button or cremini)
- 1/4 cup of onion, finely chopped
- 1 tablespoon avocado oil (for cooking)
- Salt and pepper to taste
- 1/4 cup of shredded cheese (optional, such as cheddar or feta)

Instructions:

1. In a skillet, heat avocado oil over medium heat. Add chopped onions and sliced mushrooms, cooking until softened and golden, about 5 minutes.
2. Add chopped spinach to the skillet and cook until wilted, about 2 minutes. Season with salt and pepper.
3. In a bowl, whisk together the eggs and season with a pinch of salt and pepper.
4. Pour the egg mixture into the skillet, covering the sautéed vegetables. Cook until the edges start to set, about 2-3 minutes.
5. If using cheese, sprinkle it on top of the omelet.
6. Carefully fold the omelet in half and continue to cook for another 1-2 minutes until fully set.
7. Slide the omelet onto a plate and serve immediately.

Nutritional Information (Per Serving):

- Total calories: 250
- Protein: 18g
- Fiber content: 2g
- Carbs: 6g
- Fats: 18g

Bacon-Wrapped Asparagus with Soft-Boiled Eggs

Time to Prepare: 10 minutes
Cook Time: 15 minutes
Servings: 2

List of Ingredients:

- 8 asparagus spears
- 4 slices of bacon
- 4 large eggs
- Salt and pepper to taste
- 1 tablespoon avocado oil (for drizzling)
- Optional: lemon wedges (for serving)

Instructions:

1. Preheat the oven to 400°F (200°C).
2. Trim the ends of the asparagus spears and wrap each spear with a slice of bacon, securing the ends if necessary.
3. Place the bacon-wrapped asparagus on a baking sheet and drizzle with avocado oil. Season with salt and pepper.
4. Bake in the preheated oven for 12-15 minutes, or until the bacon is crispy and the asparagus is tender.
5. Meanwhile, bring a pot of water to a gentle boil. Carefully add the eggs and boil for 6-7 minutes for soft-boiled eggs.
6. Once cooked, transfer the eggs to an ice bath for a few minutes, then peel.
7. Serve the bacon-wrapped asparagus alongside the soft-boiled eggs, and drizzle with additional avocado oil if desired. Garnish with lemon wedges.

Nutritional Information (Per Serving):

- Total calories: 320
- Protein: 20g
- Fiber content: 3g
- Carbs: 5g
- Fats: 24g

Matcha Coconut Latte

Time to Prepare: 5 minutes
Cook Time: 0 minutes
Servings: 2

List of Ingredients:

- 2 teaspoons of matcha green tea powder
- 1 cup of unsweetened coconut milk
- 1 cup of hot water (not boiling)
- 1 tablespoon monk fruit sweetener (or to taste)
- 1/2 teaspoon of vanilla extract
- Optional: shredded coconut for garnish

Instructions:

1. In a small bowl, whisk together the matcha powder and hot water until smooth and frothy, making sure there are no lumps.
2. In a saucepan, heat the unsweetened coconut milk over low heat until warm.
3. Add the monk fruit sweetener and vanilla extract to the coconut milk, stirring to combine.
4. Divide the matcha mixture between two cups.
5. Pour the warmed coconut milk over the matcha in each cup, stirring gently to combine.
6. Garnish with shredded coconut if desired and serve immediately.

Nutritional Information (Per Serving):

- Total calories: 90
- Protein: 2g
- Fiber content: 2g
- Carbs: 8g
- Fats: 6g

Blueberry-Almond Protein Smoothie

Time to Prepare: 5 minutes
Cook Time: 0 minutes
Servings: 1

List of Ingredients:

- 1 cup of unsweetened almond milk
- 1/2 cup of frozen blueberries
- 1 scoop vanilla protein powder (preferably plant-based)
- 1 tablespoon almond butter
- 1 tablespoon chia seeds
- 1/2 teaspoon of cinnamon
- Ice cubes (optional, for thickness)

Instructions:

1. In a blender, combine unsweetened almond milk, frozen blueberries, vanilla protein powder, almond butter, chia seeds, and cinnamon.
2. Blend until smooth and creamy, adding ice cubes if desired for a thicker consistency.
3. Pour into a glass and enjoy immediately.

Nutritional Information (Per Serving):

- Total calories: 290
- Protein: 20g
- Fiber content: 8g
- Carbs: 24g
- Fats: 14g

CHAPTER 2: LIGHT BITES & SNACKS

Cucumber & Smoked Salmon Roll-Ups

Time to Prepare: 10 minutes
Cook Time: 0 minutes
Servings: 2

List of Ingredients:

- 1 large cucumber
- 4 ounces smoked salmon
- 1/4 cup of cream cheese (or dairy-free alternative)
- 1 tablespoon fresh dill, chopped
- 1 tablespoon capers (optional)
- Salt and pepper to taste

Instructions:

1. Slice the cucumber lengthwise into thin strips using a mandoline or vegetable peeler.
2. In a small bowl, mix the cream cheese with chopped dill, salt, and pepper until well mixed.
3. Spread a thin layer of the dill cream cheese onto each cucumber strip.
4. Place a piece of smoked salmon on top of the cream cheese. If using capers, sprinkle a few on top of the salmon.
5. Carefully roll up each cucumber strip and secure with a toothpick if needed.
6. Arrange on a serving platter and enjoy immediately.

Nutritional Information (Per Serving):

- Total calories: 180
- Protein: 20g
- Fiber content: 2g
- Carbs: 6g
- Fats: 9g

Keto-Friendly Cheese Crisps

Time to Prepare: 5 minutes
Cook Time: 10 minutes
Servings: 4

List of Ingredients:

- 1 cup of shredded cheese (cheddar, Parmesan, or a blend)
- 1/4 teaspoon of garlic powder
- 1/4 teaspoon of onion powder
- 1/4 teaspoon of paprika (optional)
- Salt and pepper to taste
- Fresh herbs for garnish (optional)

Instructions:

1. Preheat the oven to 400°F (200°C) and line a baking sheet with parchment paper.
2. In a bowl, combine the shredded cheese, garlic powder, onion powder, paprika, salt, and pepper.
3. Drop tablespoon-sized mounds of the cheese mixture onto the prepared baking sheet, spacing them about 2 inches apart.
4. Flatten each mound slightly with the back of a spoon.
5. Bake in the preheated oven for 5-7 minutes, or until the cheese is melted and golden brown.
6. Remove from the oven and let cool for a few minutes until crisp.
7. Garnish with fresh herbs if desired and serve immediately.

Nutritional Information (Per Serving):

- Total calories: 120
- Protein: 10g
- Fiber content: 0g
- Carbs: 1g
- Fats: 9g

Zucchini Chips with Herb Dip

Time to Prepare: 10 minutes
Cook Time: 25 minutes
Servings: 4

List of Ingredients:

- 2 medium zucchinis, thinly sliced
- 2 tablespoons olive oil
- 1 teaspoon of garlic powder
- 1 teaspoon of onion powder
- Salt and pepper to taste
- 1/2 cup of sour cream (or Greek yogurt)
- 1 tablespoon fresh dill, chopped
- 1 tablespoon fresh parsley, chopped
- 1 teaspoon of lemon juice

Instructions:

1. Preheat the oven to 225°F (110°C) and line a baking sheet with parchment paper.
2. In a large bowl, toss the zucchini slices with olive oil, garlic powder, onion powder, salt, and pepper until evenly coated.
3. Arrange the zucchini slices in a single layer on the prepared baking sheet.
4. Bake in the preheated oven for 25-30 minutes, flipping halfway through, until the chips are crispy.
5. While the zucchini chips are baking, prepare the herb dip by mixing together sour cream, dill, parsley, lemon juice, salt, and pepper in a small bowl.
6. Serve the zucchini chips warm with the herb dip.

Nutritional Information (Per Serving):

- Total calories: 150
- Protein: 4g
- Fiber content: 3g
- Carbs: 6g
- Fats: 13g

Spicy Almond Butter Energy Balls

Time to Prepare: 10 minutes
Cook Time: 0 minutes
Servings: 12

List of Ingredients:

- 1 cup of almond butter
- 1/2 cup of unsweetened shredded coconut
- 1/4 cup of ground flaxseed
- 1/4 cup of chia seeds
- 1 tablespoon honey or monk fruit sweetener (to taste)
- 1/2 teaspoon of cayenne pepper (adjust for spice preference)
- 1 teaspoon of cinnamon
- 1/4 cup of dark chocolate chips (sugar-free, optional)

Instructions:

1. In a mixing bowl, combine almond butter, shredded coconut, ground flaxseed, chia seeds, honey or monk fruit sweetener, cayenne pepper, and cinnamon.
2. Mix thoroughly until all ingredients are well mixed. If using, fold in dark chocolate chips.
3. Use your hands to form the mixture into small balls, about 1 inch in diameter.
4. Place the energy balls on a plate or baking sheet and refrigerate for at least 30 minutes to firm up.
5. Once set, store in an airtight container in the refrigerator for up to a week.

Nutritional Information (Per Serving):

- Total calories: 120
- Protein: 4g
- Fiber content: 4g
- Carbs: 6g
- Fats: 10g

Roasted Garlic & Parmesan Kale Chips

Time to Prepare: 10 minutes
Cook Time: 20 minutes
Servings: 4

List of Ingredients:

- 1 bunch kale, stems removed and leaves torn into bite-sized pieces
- 2 tablespoons olive oil
- 2 cloves garlic, minced
- 1/4 cup of grated Parmesan cheese
- 1/2 teaspoon of salt
- 1/4 teaspoon of black pepper

Instructions:

1. Preheat the oven to 350°F (175°C) and line a baking sheet with parchment paper.
2. In a large bowl, combine the torn kale leaves, olive oil, minced garlic, salt, and pepper. Toss until the kale is evenly coated.
3. Spread the kale in a single layer on the prepared baking sheet.
4. Bake in the preheated oven for 10 minutes, then remove and sprinkle grated Parmesan cheese over the kale.
5. Return the baking sheet to the oven and bake for an additional 10 minutes, or until the kale is crispy and the cheese is melted.
6. Allow to cool slightly before serving.

Nutritional Information (Per Serving):

- Total calories: 120
- Protein: 5g
- Fiber content: 2g
- Carbs: 5g
- Fats: 10g

Stuffed Mini Bell Peppers with Cream Cheese

Time to Prepare: 10 minutes
Cook Time: 0 minutes
Servings: 4

List of Ingredients:

- 8 mini bell peppers, halved and seeds removed
- 1 cup of cream cheese (or dairy-free alternative)
- 1/4 cup of shredded cheddar cheese
- 1 tablespoon fresh chives, chopped
- 1 teaspoon of garlic powder
- Salt and pepper to taste
- Optional: crushed red pepper flakes for added spice

Instructions:

1. In a mixing bowl, combine cream cheese, shredded cheddar cheese, chopped chives, garlic powder, salt, and pepper. Mix until well mixed.
2. Spoon the cream cheese mixture into each half of the mini bell peppers, filling them generously.
3. If desired, sprinkle crushed red pepper flakes on top for extra heat.
4. Arrange the stuffed peppers on a serving platter and serve immediately, or refrigerate for up to 2 hours before serving.

Nutritional Information (Per Serving):

- Total calories: 180
- Protein: 6g
- Fiber content: 2g
- Carbs: 6g
- Fats: 16g

Crispy Avocado Fries

Time to Prepare: 10 minutes
Cook Time: 15 minutes
Servings: 4

List of Ingredients:

- 2 ripe avocados, sliced into wedges
- 1/2 cup of almond flour
- 1/4 cup of grated Parmesan cheese
- 1 teaspoon of garlic powder
- 1 teaspoon of paprika
- Salt and pepper to taste
- 2 large eggs, beaten
- Cooking spray or olive oil for baking

Instructions:

1. Preheat the oven to 425°F (220°C) and line a baking sheet with parchment paper.
2. In a shallow bowl, mix together almond flour, Parmesan cheese, garlic powder, paprika, salt, and pepper.
3. Dip each avocado wedge into the beaten eggs, allowing excess to drip off, then coat with the almond flour mixture, pressing gently to adhere.
4. Place the coated avocado wedges on the prepared baking sheet and lightly spray with cooking spray or drizzle with olive oil.
5. Bake in the preheated oven for 12-15 minutes or until golden and crispy, flipping halfway through.
6. Serve immediately with your favorite dipping sauce.

Nutritional Information (Per Serving):

- Total calories: 210
- Protein: 6g
- Fiber content: 5g
- Carbs: 12g
- Fats: 17g

Mini Caprese Skewers with Balsamic Glaze

Time to Prepare: 10 minutes
Cook Time: 0 minutes
Servings: 4

List of Ingredients:

- 1 pint cherry tomatoes
- 8 ounces fresh mozzarella balls (bocconcini)
- 1/4 cup of fresh basil leaves
- 1/4 cup of balsamic vinegar
- 1 tablespoon olive oil
- Salt and pepper to taste
- Skewers or toothpicks

Instructions:

1. In a small saucepan, heat balsamic vinegar over medium heat. Bring to a simmer and reduce for about 5-7 minutes, or until thickened. Remove from heat and let cool.
2. On each skewer or toothpick, thread a cherry tomato, a basil leaf, and a mozzarella ball. Repeat until all ingredients are used.
3. Arrange the skewers on a serving platter.
4. Drizzle the cooled balsamic glaze and olive oil over the skewers.
5. Season with salt and pepper to taste before serving.

Nutritional Information (Per Serving):

- Total calories: 150
- Protein: 8g
- Fiber content: 2g
- Carbs: 10g
- Fats: 10g

Cauliflower Hummus with Veggie Sticks

Time to Prepare: 10 minutes
Cook Time: 10 minutes
Servings: 4

List of Ingredients:

- 1 medium head cauliflower, cut into florets
- 2 tablespoons tahini
- 2 tablespoons olive oil
- 2 cloves garlic, minced
- 2 tablespoons lemon juice
- 1/2 teaspoon of cumin
- Salt and pepper to taste
- Assorted veggie sticks (carrots, celery, cucumber, bell peppers) for dipping

Instructions:

1. In a steamer basket over boiling water, steam the cauliflower florets for about 8-10 minutes, or until tender. Drain and let cool slightly.
2. In a food processor, combine the steamed cauliflower, tahini, olive oil, minced garlic, lemon juice, cumin, salt, and pepper. Blend until smooth and creamy.
3. Adjust seasoning to taste and add a little water if needed for a smoother consistency.
4. Transfer the hummus to a serving bowl and drizzle with additional olive oil if desired.
5. Serve with assorted veggie sticks for dipping.

Nutritional Information (Per Serving):

- Total calories: 100
- Protein: 4g
- Fiber content: 4g
- Carbs: 8g
- Fats: 7g

Deviled Eggs with Smoked Paprika

Time to Prepare: 10 minutes
Cook Time: 10 minutes
Servings: 4

List of Ingredients:

- 6 large eggs
- 1/4 cup of mayonnaise (or avocado mayo)
- 1 teaspoon of Dijon mustard
- 1 teaspoon of apple cider vinegar
- 1/2 teaspoon of smoked paprika
- Salt and pepper to taste
- Fresh chives or parsley, chopped (for garnish)

Instructions:

1. Place eggs in a saucepan and cover with water. Bring to a boil over medium-high heat. Once boiling, cover, remove from heat, and let sit for 10-12 minutes.
2. After cooking, transfer the eggs to an ice bath for 5 minutes to cool.
3. Peel the eggs and slice them in half lengthwise. Remove the yolks and place them in a mixing bowl.
4. Add mayonnaise, Dijon mustard, apple cider vinegar, smoked paprika, salt, and pepper to the egg yolks. Mix until smooth and creamy.
5. Spoon or pipe the yolk mixture back into the egg whites.
6. Garnish with chopped chives or parsley and an extra sprinkle of smoked paprika before serving.

Nutritional Information (Per Serving):

- Total calories: 140
- Protein: 6g
- Fiber content: 0g
- Carbs: 2g
- Fats: 12g

Baked Buffalo Cauliflower Bites

Time to Prepare: 10 minutes
Cook Time: 25 minutes
Servings: 4

List of Ingredients:

- 1 medium head cauliflower, cut into bite-sized florets
- 1/2 cup of almond flour
- 1/4 cup of unsweetened almond milk
- 1 teaspoon of garlic powder
- 1 teaspoon of onion powder
- 1/2 teaspoon of salt
- 1/2 teaspoon of black pepper
- 1/2 cup of buffalo sauce (check for no added sugars)
- 1 tablespoon olive oil

Instructions:

1. Preheat the oven to 450°F (230°C) and line a baking sheet with parchment paper.
2. In a large bowl, whisk together almond flour, garlic powder, onion powder, salt, and black pepper.
3. Dip each cauliflower floret into the almond milk, allowing excess to drip off, then coat in the almond flour mixture.
4. Place the coated cauliflower on the prepared baking sheet in a single layer. Drizzle with olive oil.
5. Bake in the preheated oven for 20 minutes, flipping halfway through, until golden and crispy.
6. Remove from the oven and toss the baked cauliflower with buffalo sauce until evenly coated.
7. Return to the oven for an additional 5 minutes.
8. Serve hot with celery sticks or a dairy-free ranch dip.

Nutritional Information (Per Serving):

- Total calories: 130
- Protein: 4g
- Fiber content: 4g
- Carbs: 10g
- Fats: 9g

Almond Butter and Celery Sticks

Time to Prepare: 5 minutes
Cook Time: 0 minutes
Servings: 2

List of Ingredients:

- 4 celery stalks, cut into sticks
- 1/4 cup of almond butter (preferably unsweetened)
- Optional toppings: chia seeds, cinnamon, or a drizzle of honey (use sparingly to keep low-carb)

Instructions:

1. Wash and cut the celery stalks into manageable sticks, about 3-4 inches long.
2. In a small bowl, stir the almond butter to ensure it's smooth and well-mixed.
3. Spread or dip almond butter onto each celery stick.
4. If desired, sprinkle with chia seeds, a dash of cinnamon, or a light drizzle of honey for extra flavor.
5. Serve immediately as a healthy snack or appetizer.

Nutritional Information (Per Serving):

- Total calories: 210
- Protein: 7g
- Fiber content: 6g
- Carbs: 10g
- Fats: 18g

Keto-Friendly Trail Mix with Nuts & Seeds

Time to Prepare: 5 minutes
Cook Time: 0 minutes
Servings: 4

List of Ingredients:

- 1/2 cup of almonds
- 1/2 cup of walnuts
- 1/4 cup of pumpkin seeds
- 1/4 cup of sunflower seeds
- 1/4 cup of unsweetened coconut flakes
- 1/4 teaspoon of sea salt
- Optional: 2 tablespoons sugar-free dark chocolate chips

Instructions:

1. In a large mixing bowl, combine the almonds, walnuts, pumpkin seeds, sunflower seeds, and coconut flakes.
2. If using, add the sugar-free dark chocolate chips to the mixture.
3. Sprinkle with sea salt and toss to combine evenly.
4. Store in an airtight container for up to a week.
5. Serve as a snack or a quick energy boost throughout the day.

Nutritional Information (Per Serving):

- Total calories: 280
- Protein: 10g
- Fiber content: 5g
- Carbs: 8g
- Fats: 25g

Garlic & Herb Roasted Pumpkin Seeds

Time to Prepare: 10 minutes
Cook Time: 20 minutes
Servings: 4

List of Ingredients:

- 1 cup of raw pumpkin seeds (pepitas)
- 1 tablespoon olive oil
- 1 teaspoon of garlic powder
- 1 teaspoon of onion powder
- 1 teaspoon of dried rosemary
- 1 teaspoon of dried thyme
- 1/2 teaspoon of sea salt
- Freshly ground black pepper to taste

Instructions:

1. Preheat the oven to 350°F (175°C) and line a baking sheet with parchment paper.
2. In a mixing bowl, combine the raw pumpkin seeds, olive oil, garlic powder, onion powder, rosemary, thyme, sea salt, and black pepper. Toss to coat evenly.
3. Spread the seasoned pumpkin seeds in a single layer on the prepared baking sheet.
4. Roast in the preheated oven for 15-20 minutes, stirring occasionally, until the seeds are golden brown and fragrant.
5. Remove from the oven and let cool completely before serving. Store in an airtight container.

Nutritional Information (Per Serving):

- Total calories: 180
- Protein: 9g
- Fiber content: 4g
- Carbs: 6g
- Fats: 15g

Mini Cucumber Sandwiches with Turkey & Avocado

Time to Prepare: 10 minutes
Cook Time: 0 minutes
Servings: 2

List of Ingredients:

- 1 large cucumber, sliced into 1/4-inch rounds
- 4 ounces sliced turkey breast (preferably nitrate-free)
- 1 ripe avocado, mashed
- 1 tablespoon fresh lemon juice
- Salt and pepper to taste
- Optional: fresh dill or parsley for garnish

Instructions:

1. In a bowl, mash the avocado and mix in lemon juice, salt, and pepper until smooth.
2. Lay out cucumber slices on a serving platter.
3. Spread a generous layer of the avocado mixture on half of the cucumber slices.
4. Top the avocado spread with a slice of turkey and then place another cucumber slice on top to create a sandwich.
5. Repeat until all ingredients are used.
6. If desired, garnish with fresh dill or parsley before serving.

Nutritional Information (Per Serving):

- Total calories: 210
- Protein: 18g
- Fiber content: 6g
- Carbs: 8g
- Fats: 12g

Spicy Tuna Salad Lettuce Wraps

Time to Prepare: 10 minutes
Cook Time: 0 minutes
Servings: 2

List of Ingredients:

- 1 (5-ounce) can tuna in water, drained
- 2 tablespoons mayonnaise (preferably avocado or olive oil-based)
- 1 tablespoon sriracha sauce (adjust to taste)
- 1 tablespoon chopped green onions
- 1 tablespoon chopped celery
- 1 tablespoon fresh cilantro, chopped
- Salt and pepper to taste
- 4 large lettuce leaves (such as romaine or butter lettuce)

Instructions:

1. In a mixing bowl, combine the drained tuna, mayonnaise, sriracha, green onions, celery, cilantro, salt, and pepper. Mix until well mixed.
2. Lay out the lettuce leaves on a serving platter.
3. Spoon the spicy tuna salad evenly into each lettuce leaf.
4. Roll or fold the lettuce leaves around the filling to create wraps.
5. Serve immediately, or refrigerate until ready to eat.

Nutritional Information (Per Serving):

- Total calories: 220
- Protein: 24g
- Fiber content: 2g
- Carbs: 4g
- Fats: 12g

Frozen Coconut Berry Bites

Time to Prepare: 15 minutes
Cook Time: 0 minutes
Servings: 6

List of Ingredients:

- 1 cup of unsweetened shredded coconut
- 1/2 cup of coconut cream
- 1/2 cup of mixed berries (strawberries, blueberries, raspberries)
- 2 tablespoons chia seeds
- 1 tablespoon vanilla extract
- 1 tablespoon sweetener of choice (e.g., erythritol or stevia)

Instructions:

1. In a mixing bowl, combine the coconut cream, vanilla extract, and sweetener. Mix well until smooth.
2. Stir in the unsweetened shredded coconut and chia seeds until fully mixed.
3. Line a muffin tin or silicone mold with parchment paper.
4. Spoon a layer of the coconut mixture into the bottom of each cup.
5. Add a few mixed berries on top of the coconut layer, then cover with more coconut mixture until the cups of are filled.
6. Freeze for at least 2 hours or until solid.
7. Once frozen, carefully remove the bites from the molds and store them in an airtight container in the freezer.

Nutritional Information (Per Serving):

- Total calories: 150
- Protein: 2g
- Fiber content: 5g
- Carbs: 8g
- Fats: 13g

CHAPTER 3: LUNCH

Grilled Chicken & Avocado Salad with Lime Vinaigrette

Time to Prepare: 15 minutes
Cook Time: 10 minutes
Servings: 2

List of Ingredients:

- 2 boneless, skinless chicken breasts
- 1 tablespoon olive oil
- Salt and pepper to taste
- 4 cups of mixed salad greens (spinach, arugula, romaine)
- 1 ripe avocado, sliced
- 1/2 cup of cherry tomatoes, halved
- 1/4 cup of red onion, thinly sliced
- 2 tablespoons fresh cilantro, chopped

For the Lime Vinaigrette:

- 2 tablespoons olive oil
- 1 tablespoon fresh lime juice
- 1 teaspoon of Dijon mustard
- 1/2 teaspoon of garlic powder
- Salt and pepper to taste

Instructions:

1. Preheat the grill to medium-high heat.
2. Brush the chicken breasts with olive oil and season with salt and pepper.
3. Grill the chicken for 6-7 minutes on each side, or until fully cooked and juices run clear. Remove from the grill and let rest for a few minutes before slicing.
4. In a small bowl, whisk together the olive oil, lime juice, Dijon mustard, garlic powder, salt, and pepper to make the vinaigrette.
5. In a large bowl, combine the mixed salad greens, sliced avocado, cherry tomatoes, red onion, and cilantro.
6. Top the salad with sliced grilled chicken and drizzle with lime vinaigrette before serving.

Nutritional Information (Per Serving):

- Total calories: 380
- Protein: 30g
- Fiber content: 10g
- Carbs: 12g
- Fats: 26g

Creamy Broccoli & Cheddar Soup

Time to Prepare: 10 minutes
Cook Time: 20 minutes
Servings: 4

List of Ingredients:

- 4 cups of fresh broccoli florets
- 1 tablespoon olive oil
- 1 small onion, diced
- 2 cloves garlic, minced
- 3 cups of vegetable broth (low-sodium)
- 1 cup of unsweetened almond milk
- 1 cup of shredded sharp cheddar cheese (or dairy-free alternative)
- 1 teaspoon of onion powder
- Salt and pepper to taste

Instructions:

1. In a large pot, heat the olive oil over medium heat. Add the diced onion and sauté until translucent, about 5 minutes.
2. Add the minced garlic and sauté for another minute until fragrant.
3. Add the broccoli florets and vegetable broth to the pot. Bring to a boil, then reduce heat and simmer for about 10 minutes, until the broccoli is tender.
4. Remove from heat and use an immersion blender to blend the soup until smooth, or transfer to a blender in batches.
5. Return the blended soup to the pot and stir in the almond milk, cheddar cheese, onion powder, salt, and pepper. Heat gently over low heat until the cheese is melted and the soup is warmed through.
6. Serve hot, garnished with extra cheese or fresh herbs if desired.

Nutritional Information (Per Serving):

- Total calories: 250
- Protein: 10g
- Fiber content: 5g
- Carbs: 12g
- Fats: 18g

Keto Taco Salad with Ground Turkey

Time to Prepare: 10 minutes
Cook Time: 15 minutes
Servings: 4

List of Ingredients:

- 1 pound ground turkey
- 1 tablespoon olive oil
- 1 tablespoon taco seasoning (low-sodium)
- 4 cups of mixed salad greens (romaine, spinach, arugula)
- 1 cup of cherry tomatoes, halved
- 1 cup of diced cucumber
- 1/2 cup of shredded cheddar cheese (or dairy-free alternative)
- 1 ripe avocado, diced
- 1/4 cup of black olives, sliced
- 1/4 cup of fresh cilantro, chopped
- 1/4 cup of salsa (sugar-free)
- 2 tablespoons sour cream (or dairy-free alternative)

Instructions:

1. In a large skillet, heat olive oil over medium heat. Add the ground turkey and cook until browned, breaking it apart with a spoon, about 7-10 minutes.
2. Stir in the taco seasoning and cook for an additional 2-3 minutes until well mixed. Remove from heat.
3. In a large bowl, layer the salad greens, cherry tomatoes, diced cucumber, and shredded cheese.
4. Add the cooked ground turkey on top of the salad mixture.
5. Top with diced avocado, black olives, and chopped cilantro.
6. Drizzle with salsa and sour cream before serving.

Nutritional Information (Per Serving):

- Total calories: 350
- Protein: 28g
- Fiber content: 9g
- Carbs: 10g
- Fats: 24g

Spinach & Feta Stuffed Portobello Mushrooms

Time to Prepare: 10 minutes
Cook Time: 25 minutes
Servings: 4

List of Ingredients:

- 4 large portobello mushrooms, stems removed
- 2 tablespoons olive oil
- 2 cups of fresh spinach, chopped
- 1 cup of crumbled feta cheese
- 1/4 cup of almond flour
- 2 cloves garlic, minced
- 1/4 teaspoon of red pepper flakes (optional)
- Salt and pepper to taste
- 1/4 cup of fresh parsley, chopped

Instructions:

1. Preheat the oven to 375°F (190°C).
2. In a skillet, heat olive oil over medium heat. Add the minced garlic and sauté for about 1 minute until fragrant.
3. Add the chopped spinach to the skillet and cook until wilted, about 2-3 minutes.
4. In a mixing bowl, combine the cooked spinach, feta cheese, almond flour, red pepper flakes, salt, and pepper. Mix until well mixed.
5. Place the portobello mushrooms on a baking sheet, gill side up. Fill each mushroom cap with the spinach and feta mixture, pressing down gently to pack it in.
6. Bake in the preheated oven for 20 minutes, until the mushrooms are tender and the filling is heated through.
7. Remove from the oven and sprinkle with fresh parsley before serving.

Nutritional Information (Per Serving):

- Total calories: 200
- Protein: 10g
- Fiber content: 5g
- Carbs: 8g
- Fats: 15g

Asian-Inspired Shrimp & Cabbage Stir-Fry

Time to Prepare: 10 minutes
Cook Time: 15 minutes
Servings: 4

List of Ingredients:

- 1 pound large shrimp, peeled and deveined
- 2 tablespoons sesame oil
- 4 cups of green cabbage, shredded
- 1 cup of bell peppers, thinly sliced (any color)
- 1 cup of carrots, julienned
- 3 cloves garlic, minced
- 1 tablespoon fresh ginger, minced
- 3 tablespoons low-sodium soy sauce (or coconut aminos)
- 1 tablespoon rice vinegar
- 1 teaspoon of red pepper flakes (optional)
- Salt and pepper to taste
- 2 green onions, sliced for garnish
- 1 tablespoon sesame seeds for garnish

Instructions:

1. In a large skillet or wok, heat sesame oil over medium-high heat.
2. Add minced garlic and ginger; sauté for about 1 minute until fragrant.
3. Add the shrimp and cook for 3-4 minutes, stirring frequently until they turn pink and opaque.
4. Remove the shrimp from the skillet and set aside.
5. In the same skillet, add shredded cabbage, bell peppers, and carrots. Stir-fry for about 5-6 minutes until the vegetables are tender-crisp.
6. Return the shrimp to the skillet and add the soy sauce, rice vinegar, red pepper flakes, salt, and pepper. Stir to combine and cook for an additional 2-3 minutes until heated through.
7. Remove from heat and garnish with sliced green onions and sesame seeds before serving.

Nutritional Information (Per Serving):

- Total calories: 220
- Protein: 22g
- Fiber content: 4g
- Carbs: 8g
- Fats: 10g

Cauliflower Fried "Rice" with Beef

Time to Prepare: 10 minutes
Cook Time: 15 minutes
Servings: 4

List of Ingredients:

- 1 pound ground beef (preferably lean)
- 4 cups of cauliflower rice (fresh or frozen)
- 2 tablespoons coconut oil or avocado oil
- 1 cup of green onions, chopped
- 1 cup of bell peppers, diced (any color)
- 1/2 cup of carrots, diced
- 3 cloves garlic, minced
- 2 tablespoons low-sodium soy sauce (or coconut aminos)
- 1 tablespoon sesame oil
- Salt and pepper to taste
- 1/4 cup of frozen peas (optional)

Instructions:

1. In a large skillet or wok, heat coconut oil over medium-high heat.
2. Add ground beef and cook until browned, breaking it apart with a spatula, about 5-7 minutes. Drain excess fat if necessary.
3. Add minced garlic and cook for another minute until fragrant.
4. Stir in the diced bell peppers, carrots, and green onions. Cook for about 3-4 minutes until the vegetables are tender.
5. Add cauliflower rice to the skillet, stirring well to combine. Cook for an additional 3-4 minutes, stirring frequently, until the cauliflower is heated through.
6. Pour in the soy sauce and sesame oil, mixing everything together. Season with salt and pepper to taste.
7. If using, add the frozen peas and cook for another minute until heated.
8. Remove from heat and serve hot.

Nutritional Information (Per Serving):

- Total calories: 300
- Protein: 25g
- Fiber content: 4g
- Carbs: 10g
- Fats: 20g

Lemon-Dill Salmon Lettuce Wraps

Time to Prepare: 10 minutes
Cook Time: 15 minutes
Servings: 4

List of Ingredients:

- 1 pound fresh salmon fillets
- 2 tablespoons olive oil
- 2 tablespoons fresh lemon juice
- 1 tablespoon fresh dill, chopped (or 1 teaspoon of dried dill)
- Salt and pepper to taste
- 8 large romaine or butter lettuce leaves
- 1/2 cup of cucumber, diced
- 1/2 cup of cherry tomatoes, halved
- 1 avocado, sliced
- 1/4 cup of red onion, thinly sliced

Instructions:

1. Preheat the grill or a skillet over medium-high heat.
2. In a small bowl, mix olive oil, lemon juice, dill, salt, and pepper.
3. Brush the salmon fillets with the lemon-dill mixture on both sides.
4. Grill or cook the salmon for about 4-5 minutes per side, or until cooked through and flaky.
5. While the salmon cooks, prepare the lettuce wraps by laying the lettuce leaves on a serving platter.
6. Once the salmon is done, flake it into bite-sized pieces.
7. Place a portion of salmon in each lettuce leaf, topped with diced cucumber, cherry tomatoes, avocado slices, and red onion.
8. Drizzle any remaining lemon-dill mixture over the top if desired. Serve immediately.

Nutritional Information (Per Serving):

- Total calories: 350
- Protein: 30g
- Fiber content: 6g
- Carbs: 12g
- Fats: 22g

Greek Chicken Salad with Cucumber & Olives

Time to Prepare: 15 minutes
Cook Time: 15 minutes
Servings: 4

List of Ingredients:

- 1 pound grilled chicken breast, diced
- 1 cup of cucumber, diced
- 1 cup of cherry tomatoes, halved
- 1/2 cup of Kalamata olives, pitted and halved
- 1/4 red onion, thinly sliced
- 1/2 cup of feta cheese, crumbled (optional)
- 3 tablespoons olive oil
- 2 tablespoons red wine vinegar
- 1 teaspoon of dried oregano
- Salt and pepper to taste
- Fresh parsley, chopped for garnish (optional)

Instructions:

1. In a large bowl, combine the diced grilled chicken, cucumber, cherry tomatoes, Kalamata olives, and red onion.
2. In a small bowl, whisk together olive oil, red wine vinegar, oregano, salt, and pepper.
3. Pour the dressing over the salad mixture and toss gently to combine.
4. If using, sprinkle feta cheese over the top and garnish with chopped parsley.
5. Serve immediately or chill for 30 minutes for the flavors to meld.

Nutritional Information (Per Serving):

- Total calories: 360
- Protein: 30g
- Fiber content: 4g
- Carbs: 10g
- Fats: 24g

Zucchini Noodle Alfredo with Grilled Chicken

Time to Prepare: 15 minutes
Cook Time: 15 minutes
Servings: 4

List of Ingredients:

- 4 medium zucchinis, spiralized
- 1 pound grilled chicken breast, sliced
- 1 cup of heavy cream
- 1 cup of grated Parmesan cheese
- 2 tablespoons olive oil
- 2 cloves garlic, minced
- Salt and pepper to taste
- Fresh parsley, chopped for garnish (optional)

Instructions:

1. In a large skillet, heat olive oil over medium heat. Add minced garlic and sauté for about 1 minute until fragrant.
2. Pour in the heavy cream and bring to a simmer.
3. Stir in the Parmesan cheese, salt, and pepper, mixing until the sauce is smooth and creamy.
4. Add the spiralized zucchini noodles to the skillet and toss them in the sauce. Cook for 2-3 minutes until the noodles are just tender.
5. Serve the zucchini noodles topped with sliced grilled chicken and garnish with fresh parsley, if desired.

Nutritional Information (Per Serving):

- Total calories: 420
- Protein: 35g
- Fiber content: 3g
- Carbs: 10g
- Fats: 28g

Low-Carb BLT Wraps

Time to Prepare: 10 minutes
Cook Time: 5 minutes
Servings: 4

List of Ingredients:

- 8 large romaine lettuce leaves
- 8 slices of cooked bacon
- 1 cup of diced tomatoes
- 1/2 cup of mayonnaise (preferably sugar-free)
- Salt and pepper to taste
- 1/4 teaspoon of garlic powder (optional)

Instructions:

1. Lay the romaine lettuce leaves flat on a clean surface.
2. Spread a tablespoon of mayonnaise on each leaf.
3. Place two slices of cooked bacon on top of the mayonnaise on each leaf.
4. Add diced tomatoes over the bacon and season with salt, pepper, and garlic powder if using.
5. Carefully roll each lettuce leaf up tightly to form a wrap.
6. Serve immediately or secure with toothpicks for easy handling.

Nutritional Information (Per Serving):

- Total calories: 310
- Protein: 22g
- Fiber content: 2g
- Carbs: 4g
- Fats: 24g

Garlic & Herb Roasted Veggie Bowl

Time to Prepare: 15 minutes
Cook Time: 30 minutes
Servings: 4

List of Ingredients:

- 2 cups of broccoli florets
- 1 cup of bell peppers, chopped
- 1 cup of zucchini, sliced
- 1 cup of cherry tomatoes, halved
- 1/4 cup of olive oil
- 4 cloves garlic, minced
- 1 teaspoon of dried oregano
- 1 teaspoon of dried thyme
- Salt and pepper to taste
- 1/4 cup of grated Parmesan cheese (optional)

Instructions:

1. Preheat the oven to 400°F (200°C).
2. In a large bowl, combine the broccoli, bell peppers, zucchini, and cherry tomatoes.
3. In a small bowl, whisk together the olive oil, minced garlic, oregano, thyme, salt, and pepper.
4. Pour the garlic-herb mixture over the vegetables and toss until evenly coated.
5. Spread the vegetables in a single layer on a baking sheet lined with parchment paper.
6. Roast in the preheated oven for 25-30 minutes, or until the veggies are tender and slightly caramelized.
7. If using, sprinkle with grated Parmesan cheese before serving.

Nutritional Information (Per Serving):

- Total calories: 220
- Protein: 4g
- Fiber content: 6g
- Carbs: 16g
- Fats: 18g

Curried Cauliflower Soup with Coconut Milk

Time to Prepare: 10 minutes
Cook Time: 25 minutes
Servings: 4

List of Ingredients:

- 1 medium head of cauliflower, chopped
- 1 medium onion, chopped
- 3 cloves garlic, minced
- 1 tablespoon fresh ginger, minced
- 2 tablespoons olive oil
- 2 teaspoons of curry powder
- 4 cups of vegetable broth
- 1 can (13.5 oz) coconut milk
- Salt and pepper to taste
- Fresh cilantro for garnish (optional)

Instructions:

1. In a large pot, heat olive oil over medium heat. Add the chopped onion and sauté until translucent, about 5 minutes.
2. Stir in the minced garlic and ginger, cooking for an additional minute until fragrant.
3. Add the chopped cauliflower and curry powder, stirring to coat the vegetables.
4. Pour in the vegetable broth and bring to a boil. Reduce the heat and simmer for 15-20 minutes, or until the cauliflower is tender.
5. Remove from heat and use an immersion blender to puree the soup until smooth. Alternatively, transfer the soup to a blender in batches to blend.
6. Return the pureed soup to the pot and stir in the coconut milk. Season with salt and pepper to taste.
7. Heat the soup over low heat until warmed through, then serve garnished with fresh cilantro if desired.

Nutritional Information (Per Serving):

- Total calories: 210
- Protein: 4g
- Fiber content: 5g
- Carbs: 12g
- Fats: 18g

Italian Meatball Zoodle Soup

Time to Prepare: 15 minutes
Cook Time: 30 minutes
Servings: 4

List of Ingredients:

- 1 pound ground turkey or beef
- 1/4 cup of grated Parmesan cheese
- 1/4 cup of almond flour
- 1 large egg
- 1 teaspoon of garlic powder
- 1 teaspoon of onion powder
- 1 teaspoon of Italian seasoning
- Salt and pepper to taste
- 4 cups of low-sodium chicken broth
- 1 can (14.5 oz) diced tomatoes (no added sugar)
- 2 medium zucchini, spiralized into noodles
- 2 cups of fresh spinach
- Fresh basil for garnish (optional)

Instructions:

1. In a bowl, combine the ground turkey (or beef), Parmesan cheese, almond flour, egg, garlic powder, onion powder, Italian seasoning, salt, and pepper. Mix until well mixed.
2. Roll the mixture into small meatballs (about 1 inch in diameter).
3. In a large pot, bring the chicken broth and diced tomatoes to a simmer over medium heat.
4. Carefully add the meatballs to the pot and simmer for about 15-20 minutes, until they are cooked through.
5. Add the spiralized zucchini and spinach to the pot and cook for an additional 5 minutes until the zoodles are tender.
6. Taste and adjust seasoning as needed. Serve hot, garnished with fresh basil if desired.

Nutritional Information (Per Serving):

- Total calories: 280
- Protein: 28g
- Fiber content: 4g
- Carbs: 10g
- Fats: 15g

Balsamic Chicken & Roasted Veggie Sheet Pan Meal

Time to Prepare: 15 minutes
Cook Time: 30 minutes
Servings: 4

List of Ingredients:

- 1 pound boneless, skinless chicken breasts
- 1/4 cup of balsamic vinegar
- 2 tablespoons olive oil
- 1 teaspoon of garlic powder
- 1 teaspoon of dried Italian herbs
- Salt and pepper to taste
- 2 cups of broccoli florets
- 1 cup of cherry tomatoes, halved
- 1 cup of bell peppers, sliced
- 1 medium zucchini, sliced

Instructions:

1. Preheat the oven to 400°F (200°C).
2. In a large bowl, whisk together balsamic vinegar, olive oil, garlic powder, Italian herbs, salt, and pepper.
3. Add the chicken breasts to the bowl and coat them well with the marinade. Let it marinate for 10 minutes.
4. On a large sheet pan, arrange the marinated chicken breasts and surround them with the broccoli, cherry tomatoes, bell peppers, and zucchini.
5. Drizzle any remaining marinade over the vegetables.
6. Bake in the preheated oven for 25-30 minutes or until the chicken is cooked through and the veggies are tender.
7. Serve warm, ensuring each plate has a balance of chicken and roasted veggies.

Nutritional Information (Per Serving):

- Total calories: 320
- Protein: 30g
- Fiber content: 5g
- Carbs: 12g
- Fats: 18g

Tuna & Egg Salad on Butter Lettuce

Time to Prepare: 10 minutes
Cook Time: 0 minutes
Servings: 2

List of Ingredients:

- 1 can (5 oz) tuna, drained
- 2 hard-boiled eggs, chopped
- 1/4 cup of mayonnaise (preferably avocado or olive oil-based)
- 1 tablespoon Dijon mustard
- 1 tablespoon lemon juice
- Salt and pepper to taste
- 1 tablespoon chopped fresh dill (optional)
- 4 large butter lettuce leaves

Instructions:

1. In a medium bowl, combine the drained tuna, chopped hard-boiled eggs, mayonnaise, Dijon mustard, lemon juice, salt, pepper, and dill (if using). Mix until well mixed.
2. Lay out the butter lettuce leaves on a plate.
3. Spoon the tuna and egg salad mixture onto each lettuce leaf.
4. Serve immediately as a light lunch or snack, enjoying the freshness of the lettuce with the creamy salad.

Nutritional Information (Per Serving):

- Total calories: 320
- Protein: 30g
- Fiber content: 1g
- Carbs: 3g
- Fats: 20g

Cajun Shrimp & Avocado Salad

Time to Prepare: 10 minutes
Cook Time: 5 minutes
Servings: 2

List of Ingredients:

- 1/2 lb shrimp, peeled and deveined
- 1 tablespoon olive oil
- 1 teaspoon of Cajun seasoning
- 1 avocado, diced
- 2 cups of mixed greens
- 1/2 cup of cherry tomatoes, halved
- 1/4 cup of red onion, thinly sliced
- 1 tablespoon lemon juice
- Salt and pepper to taste

Instructions:

1. In a bowl, toss shrimp with olive oil and Cajun seasoning until evenly coated.
2. Heat a skillet over medium heat and cook shrimp for 2-3 minutes per side until fully cooked. Remove from heat.
3. In a large bowl, combine mixed greens, cherry tomatoes, red onion, and diced avocado.
4. Add the cooked shrimp to the salad.
5. Drizzle with lemon juice, season with salt and pepper, and gently toss to combine.
6. Serve immediately.

Nutritional Information (Per Serving):

- Total calories: 350
- Protein: 25g
- Fiber content: 7g
- Carbs: 10g
- Fats: 22g

CHAPTER 4: DINNER

Garlic Butter Baked Salmon with Asparagus

Time to Prepare: 10 minutes
Cook Time: 15 minutes
Servings: 2

List of Ingredients:

- 2 salmon fillets (6 oz each)
- 1 bunch asparagus, trimmed
- 2 tablespoons grass-fed butter, melted
- 3 garlic cloves, minced
- 1 tablespoon lemon juice
- Salt and pepper to taste
- 1 teaspoon of fresh parsley, chopped (optional)

Instructions:

1. Preheat oven to 400°F (200°C).
2. Arrange salmon fillets and asparagus on a baking sheet.
3. In a small bowl, mix melted butter, minced garlic, and lemon juice.
4. Drizzle the garlic butter mixture over the salmon and asparagus.
5. Season with salt and pepper.
6. Bake for 12-15 minutes or until the salmon is cooked through and the asparagus is tender.
7. Garnish with chopped parsley if desired. Serve immediately.

Nutritional Information (Per Serving):

- Total calories: 450
- Protein: 35g
- Fiber content: 4g
- Carbs: 6g
- Fats: 30g

Zesty Lemon-Herb Chicken Thighs

Time to Prepare: 10 minutes
Cook Time: 25 minutes
Servings: 4

List of Ingredients:

- 4 bone-in, skin-on chicken thighs
- 2 tablespoons olive oil
- 2 tablespoons lemon juice
- 1 tablespoon lemon zest
- 3 garlic cloves, minced
- 1 teaspoon of dried oregano
- 1 teaspoon of dried thyme
- Salt and pepper to taste
- Fresh parsley, chopped (for garnish)

Instructions:

1. Preheat oven to 400°F (200°C).
2. In a bowl, mix olive oil, lemon juice, lemon zest, minced garlic, oregano, thyme, salt, and pepper.
3. Rub the mixture over the chicken thighs, ensuring even coating.
4. Place the chicken thighs on a baking sheet, skin side up.
5. Bake for 25-30 minutes or until the chicken reaches an internal temperature of 165°F (74°C).
6. Let rest for 5 minutes before serving. Garnish with fresh parsley if desired.

Nutritional Information (Per Serving):

- Total calories: 320
- Protein: 22g
- Fiber content: 0g
- Carbs: 2g
- Fats: 24g

Beef & Veggie Stir-Fry with Coconut Aminos

Time to Prepare: 10 minutes
Cook Time: 15 minutes
Servings: 4

List of Ingredients:

- 1 lb beef sirloin, thinly sliced
- 2 tablespoons coconut oil
- 1 cup of broccoli florets
- 1 red bell pepper, thinly sliced
- 1 zucchini, thinly sliced
- 2 garlic cloves, minced
- 1/4 cup of coconut aminos
- 1 teaspoon of ground ginger
- Salt and pepper to taste
- 2 green onions, sliced (for garnish)

Instructions:

1. Heat 1 tablespoon of coconut oil in a large skillet over medium-high heat. Add beef and cook until browned, about 5 minutes. Remove beef and set aside.
2. In the same skillet, add remaining coconut oil, broccoli, bell pepper, zucchini, and garlic. Sauté for 5-7 minutes until vegetables are tender.
3. Return beef to the skillet, add coconut aminos, ground ginger, salt, and pepper. Stir well and cook for an additional 2-3 minutes until everything is heated through.
4. Serve hot, garnished with sliced green onions.

Nutritional Information (Per Serving):

- Total calories: 320
- Protein: 25g
- Fiber content: 3g
- Carbs: 7g
- Fats: 20g

Sheet Pan Shrimp Fajitas

Time to Prepare: 10 minutes
Cook Time: 15 minutes
Servings: 4

List of Ingredients:

- 1 lb large shrimp, peeled and deveined
- 1 red bell pepper, thinly sliced
- 1 yellow bell pepper, thinly sliced
- 1 green bell pepper, thinly sliced
- 1 red onion, thinly sliced
- 2 tablespoons olive oil
- 1 tablespoon chili powder
- 1 teaspoon of cumin
- 1 teaspoon of smoked paprika
- 1/2 teaspoon of garlic powder
- Salt and pepper to taste
- Juice of 1 lime
- Fresh cilantro, chopped (for garnish)

Instructions:

1. Preheat the oven to 400°F (200°C).
2. On a large sheet pan, spread the shrimp, bell peppers, and red onion. Drizzle with olive oil.
3. Sprinkle with chili powder, cumin, smoked paprika, garlic powder, salt, and pepper. Toss to coat evenly.
4. Bake for 10-12 minutes, or until the shrimp are opaque and vegetables are tender.
5. Squeeze lime juice over the fajitas and garnish with fresh cilantro.
6. Serve hot with lettuce wraps or low-carb tortillas if desired.

Nutritional Information (Per Serving):

- Total calories: 220
- Protein: 24g
- Fiber content: 3g
- Carbs: 8g
- Fats: 12g

Spaghetti Squash with Pesto & Grilled Chicken

Time to Prepare: 15 minutes
Cook Time: 40 minutes
Servings: 4

List of Ingredients:

- 1 medium spaghetti squash
- 2 tablespoons olive oil, divided
- Salt and pepper, to taste
- 2 chicken breasts
- 1/2 cup of basil pesto (made with basil, olive oil, pine nuts, and Parmesan)
- 1/4 cup of grated Parmesan cheese

Instructions:

1. Preheat the oven to 400°F (200°C).
2. Cut the spaghetti squash in half lengthwise and remove the seeds. Drizzle with 1 tablespoon olive oil, and season with salt and pepper.
3. Place the squash halves cut-side down on a baking sheet and bake for 30-35 minutes, until the flesh is tender and can be shredded with a fork.
4. While the squash is baking, season the chicken breasts with salt and pepper. Grill over medium heat for 6-8 minutes per side, until fully cooked. Slice the chicken into strips.
5. Use a fork to scrape the spaghetti squash into strands.
6. Toss the squash with the pesto until evenly coated.
7. Top with grilled chicken slices and sprinkle with Parmesan cheese before serving.

Nutritional Information (Per Serving):

- Total calories: 350
- Protein: 28g
- Fiber content: 4g
- Carbs: 10g
- Fats: 22g

Cauliflower Crust Margherita Pizza

Time to Prepare: 15 minutes
Cook Time: 25 minutes
Servings: 4

List of Ingredients:

- 1 medium head of cauliflower, riced
- 1/2 cup of grated Parmesan cheese
- 1/2 cup of shredded mozzarella cheese, divided
- 1 egg
- 1/2 teaspoon of garlic powder
- Salt and pepper, to taste
- 1/2 cup of sugar-free marinara sauce
- 1/2 cup of fresh mozzarella cheese, sliced
- 1/4 cup of fresh basil leaves

Instructions:

1. Preheat the oven to 425°F (220°C) and line a baking sheet with parchment paper.
2. Steam the riced cauliflower until tender. Let it cool, then use a cheesecloth or clean towel to squeeze out as much moisture as possible.
3. In a bowl, combine the cauliflower, Parmesan, 1/4 cup of shredded mozzarella, egg, garlic powder, salt, and pepper. Mix until a dough forms.
4. Press the dough onto the prepared baking sheet, forming a thin pizza crust. Bake for 12-15 minutes, until golden brown.
5. Spread the marinara sauce evenly over the crust, then top with fresh mozzarella slices.
6. Bake for an additional 8-10 minutes, until the cheese is melted and bubbly.
7. Remove from the oven and garnish with fresh basil leaves before serving.

Nutritional Information (Per Serving):

- Total calories: 220
- Protein: 15g
- Fiber content: 3g
- Carbs: 7g
- Fats: 14g

Keto-Friendly Lasagna with Zucchini Noodles

Time to Prepare: 20 minutes
Cook Time: 45 minutes
Servings: 6

List of Ingredients:

- 3 large zucchinis, sliced lengthwise into thin strips
- 1 lb ground turkey
- 1 cup of ricotta cheese
- 1 cup of shredded mozzarella cheese, divided
- 1/2 cup of grated Parmesan cheese
- 1 egg
- 2 cups of sugar-free marinara sauce
- 1 teaspoon of garlic powder
- 1 teaspoon of Italian seasoning
- Salt and pepper, to taste

Instructions:

1. Preheat the oven to 375°F (190°C).
2. In a skillet, cook the ground turkey over medium heat until browned. Add salt, pepper, and garlic powder. Stir in the marinara sauce and set aside.
3. In a bowl, combine ricotta cheese, egg, Parmesan, Italian seasoning, and half of the shredded mozzarella. Mix until smooth.
4. In a 9x13-inch baking dish, layer a third of the zucchini slices, followed by half of the turkey mixture, and then half of the ricotta mixture. Repeat layers, ending with a final layer of zucchini slices.
5. Top with the remaining shredded mozzarella cheese.
6. Cover with foil and bake for 25 minutes. Remove the foil and bake for an additional 15-20 minutes, until the cheese is bubbly and golden.
7. Let the lasagna rest for 10 minutes before serving.

Nutritional Information (Per Serving):

- Total calories: 320
- Protein: 24g
- Fiber content: 2g
- Carbs: 8g
- Fats: 20g

Seared Ahi Tuna with Ginger-Cucumber Slaw

Time to Prepare: 15 minutes
Cook Time: 5 minutes
Servings: 2

List of Ingredients:

- 2 ahi tuna steaks (about 6 oz each)
- 1 tablespoon coconut aminos
- 1 teaspoon of sesame oil
- 1 teaspoon of fresh ginger, minced
- 1 tablespoon olive oil
- Salt and pepper, to taste
- 1 cucumber, julienned
- 1 carrot, julienned
- 1/4 cup of red cabbage, thinly sliced
- 1 tablespoon rice vinegar
- 1 teaspoon of sesame seeds

Instructions:

1. Rub the tuna steaks with coconut aminos, sesame oil, salt, and pepper.
2. Heat olive oil in a skillet over high heat. Sear tuna for 1-2 minutes on each side for a medium-rare center. Remove from the skillet and let rest.
3. In a bowl, combine cucumber, carrot, red cabbage, rice vinegar, and fresh ginger. Mix well.
4. Slice the seared tuna and serve over the ginger-cucumber slaw. Sprinkle with sesame seeds before serving.

Nutritional Information (Per Serving):

- Total calories: 280
- Protein: 32g
- Fiber content: 3g
- Carbs: 7g
- Fats: 12g

Rosemary-Garlic Pork Tenderloin

Time to Prepare: 10 minutes
Cook Time: 25 minutes
Servings: 4

List of Ingredients:

- 1 pork tenderloin (about 1 lb)
- 2 tablespoons olive oil
- 3 garlic cloves, minced
- 2 teaspoons of fresh rosemary, chopped
- Salt and pepper, to taste

Instructions:

1. Preheat oven to 400°F (200°C).
2. In a small bowl, mix olive oil, garlic, rosemary, salt, and pepper. Rub the mixture evenly over the pork tenderloin.
3. Heat a skillet over medium-high heat and sear the pork tenderloin on all sides until browned (about 2-3 minutes per side).
4. Transfer the seared tenderloin to a baking dish and roast in the oven for 15-20 minutes or until the internal temperature reaches 145°F (63°C).
5. Remove from the oven, cover with foil, and let rest for 5 minutes before slicing.

Nutritional Information (Per Serving):

- Total calories: 240
- Protein: 28g
- Fiber content: 0g
- Carbs: 1g
- Fats: 14g

Miso Cod with Bok Choy

Time to Prepare: 15 minutes
Cook Time: 20 minutes
Servings: 4

List of Ingredients:

- 4 cod fillets (6 oz each)
- 1/4 cup of white miso paste
- 2 tablespoons rice vinegar
- 2 tablespoons coconut aminos
- 1 tablespoon sesame oil
- 2 cloves garlic, minced
- 4 cups of bok choy, halved
- 1 tablespoon olive oil
- Salt and pepper, to taste
- 1 tablespoon sesame seeds (for garnish)

Instructions:

1. In a bowl, whisk together miso paste, rice vinegar, coconut aminos, sesame oil, and garlic to make the marinade.
2. Place the cod fillets in a shallow dish and pour the marinade over them. Let marinate for at least 15 minutes.
3. Preheat the oven to 400°F (200°C).
4. On a baking sheet, arrange the marinated cod fillets and roast for 12-15 minutes, or until cooked through and flaky.
5. Meanwhile, heat olive oil in a skillet over medium heat. Add bok choy, season with salt and pepper, and sauté for about 5-7 minutes until tender.
6. Serve the miso cod over sautéed bok choy, garnished with sesame seeds.

Nutritional Information (Per Serving):

- Total calories: 290
- Protein: 28g
- Fiber content: 2g
- Carbs: 8g
- Fats: 16g

Chicken & Mushroom Creamy Cauliflower Rice

Time to Prepare: 10 minutes
Cook Time: 20 minutes
Servings: 4

List of Ingredients:

- 1 lb (450g) chicken breast, diced
- 2 cups of cauliflower rice
- 1 cup of mushrooms, sliced
- 1/2 cup of heavy cream (or coconut cream)
- 2 tablespoons olive oil
- 2 cloves garlic, minced
- 1 teaspoon of onion powder
- 1 teaspoon of dried thyme
- Salt and pepper, to taste
- Fresh parsley, chopped (for garnish)

Instructions:

1. Heat olive oil in a large skillet over medium heat. Add diced chicken and cook until browned and cooked through, about 5-7 minutes.
2. Add garlic and sliced mushrooms to the skillet, cooking for an additional 3-4 minutes until the mushrooms are tender.
3. Stir in cauliflower rice, heavy cream, onion powder, thyme, salt, and pepper. Cook for another 5 minutes until heated through and creamy.
4. Garnish with fresh parsley before serving.

Nutritional Information (Per Serving):

- Total calories: 380
- Protein: 34g
- Fiber content: 4g
- Carbs: 10g
- Fats: 22g

Greek-Inspired Lamb Burgers with Tzatziki Sauce

Time to Prepare: 15 minutes
Cook Time: 15 minutes
Servings: 4

List of Ingredients:

- 1 lb (450g) ground lamb
- 1/4 cup of onion, finely chopped
- 2 cloves garlic, minced
- 1 teaspoon of dried oregano
- 1 teaspoon of ground cumin
- Salt and pepper, to taste
- 1/4 cup of fresh parsley, chopped
- 1 cup of cucumber, grated
- 1/2 cup of plain Greek yogurt (or unsweetened coconut yogurt)
- 1 tablespoon lemon juice
- 1 tablespoon olive oil

Instructions:

1. In a mixing bowl, combine ground lamb, chopped onion, garlic, oregano, cumin, salt, pepper, and parsley. Mix well and form into 4 patties.
2. Preheat a grill or skillet over medium-high heat. Cook the lamb burgers for about 5-7 minutes on each side or until cooked to your desired doneness.
3. While the burgers are cooking, prepare the tzatziki sauce by mixing grated cucumber, Greek yogurt, lemon juice, olive oil, salt, and pepper in a bowl.
4. Serve the lamb burgers topped with tzatziki sauce.

Nutritional Information (Per Serving):

- Total calories: 430
- Protein: 28g
- Fiber content: 2g
- Carbs: 6g
- Fats: 34g

Slow-Cooked Beef Stew with Root Vegetables

Time to Prepare: 20 minutes
Cook Time: 8 hours (slow cooker)
Servings: 6

List of Ingredients:

- 2 lbs (900g) beef chuck, cut into 1-inch cubes
- 1 large onion, chopped
- 3 cloves garlic, minced
- 4 cups of low-sodium beef broth
- 2 cups of carrots, diced
- 2 cups of celery, diced
- 1 cup of turnips, diced
- 1 teaspoon of dried thyme
- 1 teaspoon of dried rosemary
- Salt and pepper, to taste
- 2 tablespoons olive oil

Instructions:

1. In a large skillet, heat olive oil over medium-high heat. Add the beef cubes and brown on all sides.
2. Transfer the browned beef to a slow cooker. Add chopped onion, minced garlic, carrots, celery, turnips, thyme, rosemary, salt, pepper, and beef broth.
3. Stir to combine, then cover and cook on low for 8 hours or until the beef is tender and vegetables are cooked through.
4. Adjust seasoning as needed before serving.

Nutritional Information (Per Serving):

- Total calories: 330
- Protein: 35g
- Fiber content: 4g
- Carbs: 10g
- Fats: 15g

Stuffed Bell Peppers with Ground Turkey & Veggies

Time to Prepare: 15 minutes
Cook Time: 30 minutes
Servings: 4

List of Ingredients:

- 4 large bell peppers (any color)
- 1 lb (450g) ground turkey
- 1 small onion, chopped
- 2 cloves garlic, minced
- 1 cup of zucchini, diced
- 1 cup of diced tomatoes (canned or fresh)
- 1 teaspoon of Italian seasoning
- 1 teaspoon of paprika
- Salt and pepper, to taste
- 1 tablespoon olive oil
- 1 cup of shredded mozzarella cheese (optional)

Instructions:

1. Preheat the oven to 375°F (190°C).
2. Cut the tops off the bell peppers and remove the seeds. Place the peppers upright in a baking dish.
3. In a skillet, heat olive oil over medium heat. Add the chopped onion and minced garlic, sautéing until soft.
4. Add the ground turkey, zucchini, diced tomatoes, Italian seasoning, paprika, salt, and pepper to the skillet. Cook until the turkey is browned and cooked through.
5. Stuff the mixture into the hollowed bell peppers. If using, sprinkle mozzarella cheese on top of each pepper.
6. Cover the baking dish with foil and bake for 25 minutes. Remove the foil and bake for an additional 5-10 minutes until the peppers are tender and cheese is bubbly.
7. Serve hot.

Nutritional Information (Per Serving):

- Total calories: 280
- Protein: 30g
- Fiber content: 5g
- Carbs: 12g
- Fats: 12g

Roasted Lemon-Garlic Brussels Sprouts & Sausage

Time to Prepare: 10 minutes
Cook Time: 25 minutes
Servings: 4

List of Ingredients:

- 1 lb (450g) Brussels sprouts, trimmed and halved
- 1 lb (450g) sausage (Italian or chicken sausage)
- 3 tablespoons olive oil
- 3 cloves garlic, minced
- Juice and zest of 1 lemon
- Salt and pepper, to taste
- 1 teaspoon of dried thyme or rosemary

Instructions:

1. Preheat the oven to 400°F (200°C).
2. In a large mixing bowl, combine Brussels sprouts, sliced sausage, olive oil, minced garlic, lemon juice, lemon zest, salt, pepper, and thyme or rosemary. Toss until evenly coated.
3. Spread the mixture onto a baking sheet in a single layer.
4. Roast for 20-25 minutes, stirring halfway through, until Brussels sprouts are tender and sausages are browned.
5. Remove from the oven and serve hot.

Nutritional Information (Per Serving):

- Total calories: 350
- Protein: 22g
- Fiber content: 6g
- Carbs: 12g
- Fats: 24g

Thai-Inspired Coconut Curry Chicken

Time to Prepare: 10 minutes
Cook Time: 30 minutes
Servings: 4

List of Ingredients:

- 1 lb (450g) boneless, skinless chicken thighs, cut into bite-sized pieces
- 1 can (13.5 oz) coconut milk
- 2 tablespoons red curry paste
- 1 tablespoon olive oil
- 1 cup of bell peppers, sliced (any color)
- 1 cup of zucchini, sliced
- 1 cup of broccoli florets
- 2 cloves garlic, minced
- 1 tablespoon fresh ginger, minced
- 2 tablespoons lime juice
- Salt and pepper, to taste
- Fresh cilantro, for garnish

Instructions:

1. In a large skillet, heat olive oil over medium heat.
2. Add garlic and ginger; sauté for 1-2 minutes until fragrant.
3. Add chicken and cook until browned, about 5-7 minutes.
4. Stir in the red curry paste and cook for an additional minute.
5. Pour in the coconut milk and bring to a simmer.
6. Add bell peppers, zucchini, and broccoli; cook until vegetables are tender, about 10 minutes.
7. Stir in lime juice, and season with salt and pepper.
8. Serve hot, garnished with fresh cilantro.

Nutritional Information (Per Serving):

- Total calories: 400
- Protein: 28g
- Fiber content: 5g
- Carbs: 10g
- Fats: 30g

Herbed Butter Roasted Whole Chicken

Time to Prepare: 15 minutes
Cook Time: 1 hour 30 minutes
Servings: 6

List of Ingredients:

- 1 whole chicken (about 4-5 lbs)
- 1/2 cup of unsalted butter, softened
- 2 tablespoons fresh rosemary, chopped
- 2 tablespoons fresh thyme, chopped
- 2 tablespoons fresh parsley, chopped
- 4 cloves garlic, minced
- 1 tablespoon lemon juice
- Salt and pepper, to taste
- 1 lemon, quartered
- 1 onion, quartered

Instructions:

1. Preheat the oven to 425°F (220°C).
2. In a bowl, mix the softened butter with rosemary, thyme, parsley, garlic, lemon juice, salt, and pepper until well mixed.
3. Pat the chicken dry with paper towels. Gently lift the skin and spread some of the herb butter mixture underneath. Rub the remaining butter all over the outside of the chicken.
4. Stuff the cavity of the chicken with lemon and onion quarters.
5. Place the chicken on a roasting pan and roast in the preheated oven for 1 hour and 20 minutes, or until the internal temperature reaches 165°F (74°C) and the skin is golden brown.
6. Let the chicken rest for 10-15 minutes before carving. Serve warm.

Nutritional Information (Per Serving):

- Total calories: 420
- Protein: 40g
- Fiber content: 0g
- Carbs: 1g
- Fats: 28g

CHAPTER 5: VEGGIES & SIDES

Garlic Parmesan Roasted Broccoli

Time to Prepare: 10 minutes
Cook Time: 20 minutes
Servings: 4

List of Ingredients:

- 4 cups of broccoli florets
- 3 tablespoons olive oil
- 4 cloves garlic, minced
- 1/4 cup of grated Parmesan cheese
- Salt and pepper, to taste
- 1 teaspoon of lemon juice

Instructions:

1. Preheat the oven to 425°F (220°C).
2. In a large bowl, combine broccoli florets, olive oil, minced garlic, salt, and pepper. Toss until the broccoli is evenly coated.
3. Spread the broccoli mixture in a single layer on a baking sheet.
4. Roast in the preheated oven for 15-20 minutes, or until the broccoli is tender and slightly crispy.
5. Remove from the oven and sprinkle with grated Parmesan cheese and a squeeze of lemon juice. Toss gently and serve immediately.

Nutritional Information (Per Serving):

- Total calories: 150
- Protein: 5g
- Fiber content: 4g
- Carbs: 8g
- Fats: 12g

Spicy Cauliflower Rice Pilaf

Time to Prepare: 10 minutes
Cook Time: 15 minutes
Servings: 4

List of Ingredients:

- 1 medium head cauliflower, grated into rice-sized pieces
- 2 tablespoons olive oil
- 1 small onion, diced
- 2 cloves garlic, minced
- 1 bell pepper, diced
- 1 teaspoon of smoked paprika
- 1 teaspoon of cayenne pepper (adjust to taste)
- Salt and pepper, to taste
- 1/2 cup of diced tomatoes (fresh or canned)
- 1/4 cup of chopped fresh cilantro

Instructions:

1. Heat olive oil in a large skillet over medium heat. Add the diced onion and bell pepper; sauté until softened, about 3-4 minutes.
2. Stir in the minced garlic, smoked paprika, cayenne pepper, salt, and pepper, cooking for an additional minute until fragrant.
3. Add the grated cauliflower to the skillet, stirring to combine with the other ingredients. Cook for 5-7 minutes, until the cauliflower is tender but still has some texture.
4. Stir in the diced tomatoes and cook for another 2-3 minutes until heated through.
5. Remove from heat and mix in the chopped cilantro. Serve warm.

Nutritional Information (Per Serving):

- Total calories: 120
- Protein: 4g
- Fiber content: 4g
- Carbs: 8g
- Fats: 8g

Balsamic Glazed Brussels Sprouts with Pecans

Time to Prepare: 10 minutes
Cook Time: 20 minutes
Servings: 4

List of Ingredients:

- 1 lb Brussels sprouts, halved
- 2 tablespoons olive oil
- Salt and pepper, to taste
- 1/4 cup of balsamic vinegar
- 1/4 cup of pecans, chopped
- 1 teaspoon of honey (optional for sweetness, can be omitted)

Instructions:

1. Preheat the oven to 400°F (200°C).
2. In a large bowl, toss the halved Brussels sprouts with olive oil, salt, and pepper until evenly coated.
3. Spread the Brussels sprouts on a baking sheet in a single layer. Roast in the preheated oven for 15 minutes.
4. Remove the baking sheet from the oven, drizzle the balsamic vinegar over the Brussels sprouts, and sprinkle with chopped pecans.
5. Return to the oven and roast for an additional 5 minutes, until the Brussels sprouts are tender and caramelized.
6. If using, drizzle with honey before serving.

Nutritional Information (Per Serving):

- Total calories: 150
- Protein: 4g
- Fiber content: 5g
- Carbs: 12g
- Fats: 10g

Zoodles with Sun-Dried Tomato & Olive Tapenade

Time to Prepare: 10 minutes
Cook Time: 5 minutes
Servings: 2

List of Ingredients:

- 2 medium zucchini, spiralized (zoodles)
- 1/2 cup of sun-dried tomatoes, chopped
- 1/4 cup of olives (black or green), chopped
- 2 tablespoons olive oil
- 1 clove garlic, minced
- 1 tablespoon fresh basil, chopped
- Salt and pepper, to taste
- Grated Parmesan cheese (optional, can be omitted)

Instructions:

1. Heat olive oil in a skillet over medium heat. Add minced garlic and sauté for 1 minute until fragrant.
2. Add the sun-dried tomatoes and olives to the skillet, cooking for an additional 2 minutes.
3. Add the spiralized zucchini to the skillet and toss to combine. Cook for 2-3 minutes until the zoodles are just tender.
4. Season with salt, pepper, and fresh basil. Toss to combine.
5. Serve immediately, topped with grated Parmesan cheese if desired.

Nutritional Information (Per Serving):

- Total calories: 200
- Protein: 5g
- Fiber content: 4g
- Carbs: 14g
- Fats: 15g

Grilled Asparagus with Lemon Zest

Time to Prepare: 10 minutes
Cook Time: 10 minutes
Servings: 4

List of Ingredients:

- 1 pound fresh asparagus, trimmed
- 2 tablespoons olive oil
- Zest of 1 lemon
- 1 tablespoon fresh lemon juice
- Salt and pepper, to taste
- 1 clove garlic, minced (optional)

Instructions:

1. Preheat the grill to medium-high heat.
2. In a large bowl, toss the asparagus with olive oil, lemon zest, lemon juice, salt, pepper, and minced garlic (if using).
3. Place the asparagus on the grill in a single layer. Grill for 5-7 minutes, turning occasionally, until tender and lightly charred.
4. Remove from the grill and serve warm.

Nutritional Information (Per Serving):

- Total calories: 80
- Protein: 3g
- Fiber content: 3g
- Carbs: 6g
- Fats: 6g

Roasted Rainbow Carrots with Thyme

Time to Prepare: 10 minutes
Cook Time: 30 minutes
Servings: 4

List of Ingredients:

- 1 pound rainbow carrots, peeled and cut into sticks
- 2 tablespoons olive oil
- 1 tablespoon fresh thyme leaves (or 1 teaspoon of dried thyme)
- Salt and pepper, to taste

Instructions:

1. Preheat the oven to 425°F (220°C).
2. In a large bowl, toss the carrot sticks with olive oil, thyme, salt, and pepper until evenly coated.
3. Spread the carrots in a single layer on a baking sheet.
4. Roast in the oven for 25-30 minutes, or until tender and slightly caramelized, turning halfway through.
5. Remove from the oven and serve warm.

Nutritional Information (Per Serving):

- Total calories: 110
- Protein: 1g
- Fiber content: 3g
- Carbs: 11g
- Fats: 7g

Crispy Baked Kale with Sea Salt

Time to Prepare: 10 minutes
Cook Time: 15 minutes
Servings: 4

List of Ingredients:

- 1 bunch kale, stems removed and leaves torn into pieces
- 1 tablespoon olive oil
- 1/2 teaspoon of sea salt

Instructions:

1. Preheat the oven to 350°F (175°C).
2. In a large bowl, toss the kale pieces with olive oil and sea salt until well coated.
3. Spread the kale evenly on a baking sheet lined with parchment paper.
4. Bake for 12-15 minutes, or until the edges are crispy but not burned.
5. Remove from the oven and let cool slightly before serving.

Nutritional Information (Per Serving):

- Total calories: 70
- Protein: 3g
- Fiber content: 2g
- Carbs: 10g
- Fats: 4g

Cheesy Cauliflower Mash

Time to Prepare: 10 minutes
Cook Time: 15 minutes
Servings: 4

List of Ingredients:

- 1 head cauliflower, cut into florets
- 1/2 cup of shredded cheddar cheese
- 1/4 cup of cream cheese
- 1 tablespoon butter
- 1/2 teaspoon of garlic powder
- Salt and pepper to taste

Instructions:

1. Steam or boil the cauliflower florets until tender, about 10-12 minutes.
2. Drain well and transfer to a large bowl.
3. Add the cheddar cheese, cream cheese, butter, garlic powder, salt, and pepper.
4. Use an immersion blender or a potato masher to blend the cauliflower until smooth and creamy.
5. Taste and adjust seasoning if necessary. Serve warm.

Nutritional Information (Per Serving):

- Total calories: 140
- Protein: 6g
- Fiber content: 4g
- Carbs: 8g
- Fats: 10g

Spicy Sautéed Spinach with Garlic

Time to Prepare: 5 minutes
Cook Time: 5 minutes
Servings: 4

List of Ingredients:

- 10 ounces fresh spinach
- 2 tablespoons olive oil
- 3 cloves garlic, minced
- 1/2 teaspoon of red pepper flakes
- Salt and pepper to taste
- Juice of 1/2 lemon

Instructions:

1. Heat the olive oil in a large skillet over medium heat.
2. Add the minced garlic and red pepper flakes, sautéing for about 30 seconds until fragrant.
3. Add the fresh spinach to the skillet and cook, stirring frequently, until wilted, about 3-4 minutes.
4. Season with salt, pepper, and lemon juice. Serve immediately.

Nutritional Information (Per Serving):

- Total calories: 120
- Protein: 3g
- Fiber content: 2g
- Carbs: 6g
- Fats: 10g

Buttery Cabbage Steaks

Time to Prepare: 10 minutes
Cook Time: 25 minutes
Servings: 4

List of Ingredients:

- 1 medium head of cabbage
- 4 tablespoons unsalted butter, melted
- 1 teaspoon of garlic powder
- 1 teaspoon of onion powder
- Salt and pepper to taste
- 1 tablespoon fresh parsley, chopped (for garnish)

Instructions:

1. Preheat the oven to 400°F (200°C).
2. Remove the outer leaves of the cabbage and slice it into 1-inch thick steaks.
3. Place the cabbage steaks on a baking sheet lined with parchment paper.
4. In a small bowl, mix the melted butter, garlic powder, onion powder, salt, and pepper.
5. Brush both sides of the cabbage steaks with the butter mixture.
6. Roast in the oven for 20-25 minutes, flipping halfway through, until golden brown and tender.
7. Garnish with chopped parsley before serving.

Nutritional Information (Per Serving):

- Total calories: 140
- Protein: 2g
- Fiber content: 4g
- Carbs: 10g
-
- Fats: 10g

Cauliflower "Mac & Cheese"

Time to Prepare: 10 minutes
Cook Time: 25 minutes
Servings: 4

List of Ingredients:

- 1 large head of cauliflower, cut into florets
- 1 cup of heavy cream
- 1 cup of shredded cheddar cheese
- 1/2 cup of cream cheese, softened
- 1/2 teaspoon of garlic powder
- 1/2 teaspoon of onion powder
- Salt and pepper to taste
- 1/4 teaspoon of smoked paprika (optional)
- 1/4 cup of grated Parmesan cheese (for topping)

Instructions:

1. Preheat the oven to 350°F (175°C).
2. Steam the cauliflower florets until tender, about 5-7 minutes.
3. In a mixing bowl, combine the heavy cream, cheddar cheese, cream cheese, garlic powder, onion powder, salt, pepper, and smoked paprika. Mix until smooth.
4. Add the steamed cauliflower to the cheese mixture and stir to combine.
5. Transfer the mixture to a greased baking dish.
6. Sprinkle the grated Parmesan cheese on top.
7. Bake in the oven for 20 minutes or until bubbly and golden.
8. Let it cool for a few minutes before serving.

Nutritional Information (Per Serving):

- Total calories: 290
- Protein: 10g
- Fiber content: 3g
- Carbs: 8g
- Fats: 25g

Roasted Radishes with Rosemary

Time to Prepare: 10 minutes
Cook Time: 25 minutes
Servings: 4

List of Ingredients:

- 1 pound radishes, halved
- 2 tablespoons olive oil
- 1 teaspoon of fresh rosemary, chopped (or 1/2 teaspoon of dried)
- Salt and pepper to taste

Instructions:

1. Preheat the oven to 425°F (220°C).
2. In a large bowl, toss the halved radishes with olive oil, rosemary, salt, and pepper until evenly coated.
3. Spread the radishes in a single layer on a baking sheet.
4. Roast in the oven for 20-25 minutes, or until the radishes are tender and golden, stirring halfway through.
5. Remove from the oven and let cool slightly before serving.

Nutritional Information (Per Serving):

- Total calories: 120
- Protein: 2g
- Fiber content: 4g
- Carbs: 7g
- Fats: 10g

Creamy Avocado & Cucumber Salad

Time to Prepare: 10 minutes
Cook Time: 0 minutes
Servings: 4

List of Ingredients:

- 2 ripe avocados, diced
- 1 large cucumber, diced
- 1/4 cup of Greek yogurt (or dairy-free yogurt)
- 1 tablespoon lemon juice
- Salt and pepper to taste
- 1 tablespoon fresh dill, chopped (optional)

Instructions:

1. In a large bowl, combine the diced avocados and cucumbers.
2. In a separate small bowl, mix the Greek yogurt, lemon juice, salt, and pepper until smooth.
3. Pour the yogurt mixture over the avocado and cucumber, then gently toss to combine.
4. If using, sprinkle the chopped dill on top and serve immediately.

Nutritional Information (Per Serving):

- Total calories: 180
- Protein: 4g
- Fiber content: 7g
- Carbs: 12g
- Fats: 14g

Sautéed Mushrooms with Fresh Herbs

Time to Prepare: 10 minutes
Cook Time: 10 minutes
Servings: 4

List of Ingredients:

- 16 oz (450g) mushrooms, sliced
- 2 tablespoons olive oil
- 3 cloves garlic, minced
- 1 teaspoon of fresh thyme, chopped
- 1 teaspoon of fresh parsley, chopped
- Salt and pepper to taste

Instructions:

1. Heat the olive oil in a large skillet over medium heat.
2. Add the sliced mushrooms and sauté for about 5-7 minutes, until they begin to soften.
3. Add the minced garlic, thyme, and parsley, and continue to sauté for an additional 3-5 minutes until the mushrooms are fully cooked and fragrant.
4. Season with salt and pepper to taste, then serve warm.

Nutritional Information (Per Serving):

- Total calories: 130
- Protein: 3g
- Fiber content: 2g
- Carbs: 6g
- Fats: 11g

Baked Zucchini Fries

Time to Prepare: 10 minutes
Cook Time: 25 minutes
Servings: 4

List of Ingredients:

- 2 medium zucchinis, cut into fries
- 1/2 cup of almond flour
- 1/2 cup of grated Parmesan cheese
- 1 teaspoon of garlic powder
- 1 teaspoon of paprika
- Salt and pepper to taste
- 2 large eggs, beaten

Instructions:

1. Preheat the oven to 425°F (220°C) and line a baking sheet with parchment paper.
2. In a shallow bowl, mix the almond flour, Parmesan cheese, garlic powder, paprika, salt, and pepper.
3. Dip each zucchini fry in the beaten eggs, then coat with the almond flour mixture.
4. Place the coated fries on the prepared baking sheet in a single layer.
5. Bake for 20-25 minutes, turning halfway through, until golden and crispy.
6. Serve immediately with your favorite dipping sauce.

Nutritional Information (Per Serving):

- Total calories: 150
- Protein: 7g
- Fiber content: 3g
- Carbs: 6g
- Fats: 12g

Garlic Lemon Green Beans

Time to Prepare: 10 minutes
Cook Time: 10 minutes
Servings: 4

List of Ingredients:

- 1 pound fresh green beans, trimmed
- 2 tablespoons olive oil
- 3 cloves garlic, minced
- Juice of 1 lemon
- Zest of 1 lemon
- Salt and pepper to taste

Instructions:

1. In a large pot, bring water to a boil. Add the green beans and blanch for 2-3 minutes until bright green and tender-crisp. Drain and set aside.
2. In a large skillet, heat the olive oil over medium heat. Add the minced garlic and sauté for about 1 minute until fragrant.
3. Add the blanched green beans to the skillet and toss to coat with the garlic oil.
4. Squeeze the lemon juice over the beans and add the lemon zest. Season with salt and pepper to taste.
5. Cook for an additional 2-3 minutes, stirring frequently, until the green beans are heated through.
6. Serve warm.

Nutritional Information (Per Serving):

- Total calories: 100
- Protein: 2g
- Fiber content: 4g
- Carbs: 9g
- Fats: 7g

Sweet & Spicy Roasted Butternut Squash

Time to Prepare: 15 minutes
Cook Time: 30 minutes
Servings: 4

List of Ingredients:

- 1 medium butternut squash, peeled and diced
- 2 tablespoons olive oil
- 2 tablespoons honey or sugar-free sweetener
- 1 teaspoon of chili powder
- 1 teaspoon of cinnamon
- Salt and pepper to taste

Instructions:

1. Preheat the oven to 400°F (200°C).
2. In a large bowl, combine the diced butternut squash, olive oil, honey (or sweetener), chili powder, cinnamon, salt, and pepper. Toss until the squash is evenly coated.
3. Spread the squash in a single layer on a baking sheet lined with parchment paper.
4. Roast in the preheated oven for 25-30 minutes, stirring halfway through, until the squash is tender and caramelized.
5. Serve warm as a side dish.

Nutritional Information (Per Serving):

- Total calories: 130
- Protein: 2g
- Fiber content: 4g
- Carbs: 25g
- Fats: 5g

CHAPTER 6: DESSERTS & SWEET TREATS

Keto Chocolate Mousse with Coconut Cream

Time to Prepare: 15 minutes
Cook Time: 0 minutes
Servings: 4

List of Ingredients:

- 1 cup of heavy cream
- 1/4 cup of unsweetened cocoa powder
- 1/4 cup of sugar-free sweetener (like erythritol)
- 1 teaspoon of vanilla extract
- 1 cup of coconut cream (chilled)
- Pinch of salt

Instructions:

1. In a medium bowl, whip the heavy cream until soft peaks form.
2. In a separate bowl, combine cocoa powder, sugar-free sweetener, vanilla extract, and a pinch of salt. Mix well.
3. Gradually fold the cocoa mixture into the whipped cream until fully incorporated.
4. Gently fold in the chilled coconut cream until smooth and creamy.
5. Spoon the mousse into serving dishes and refrigerate for at least 30 minutes before serving.

Nutritional Information (Per Serving):

- Total calories: 210
- Protein: 3g
- Fiber content: 2g
- Carbs: 6g
- Fats: 20g

Almond Flour Shortbread Cookies

Time to Prepare: 10 minutes
Cook Time: 15 minutes
Servings: 12

List of Ingredients:

- 2 cups of almond flour
- 1/4 cup of coconut oil (melted)
- 1/4 cup of sugar-free sweetener (like erythritol)
- 1 teaspoon of vanilla extract
- 1/4 teaspoon of salt
- 1 large egg (optional for binding)

Instructions:

1. Preheat the oven to 350°F (175°C) and line a baking sheet with parchment paper.
2. In a bowl, combine almond flour, melted coconut oil, sugar-free sweetener, vanilla extract, and salt. Mix until a dough forms.
3. If using, add the egg and mix until fully incorporated.
4. Roll the dough into small balls and flatten them into cookie shapes on the prepared baking sheet.
5. Bake for 12-15 minutes or until the edges are golden.
6. Remove from the oven and let cool on a wire rack before serving.

Nutritional Information (Per Serving):

- Total calories: 120
- Protein: 3g
- Fiber content: 2g
- Carbs: 5g
- Fats: 10g

Baked Cinnamon Apples with Walnuts

Time to Prepare: 10 minutes
Cook Time: 25 minutes
Servings: 4

List of Ingredients:

- 4 medium-sized apples (such as Granny Smith or Fuji)
- 1/2 cup of walnuts (chopped)
- 2 tablespoons coconut oil (melted)
- 2 teaspoons of cinnamon
- 1 tablespoon sugar-free sweetener (like erythritol or monk fruit)
- 1/4 teaspoon of salt
- 1 teaspoon of vanilla extract

Instructions:

1. Preheat the oven to 350°F (175°C) and grease a baking dish with coconut oil.
2. Core the apples and slice them into wedges, then place them in the prepared baking dish.
3. In a bowl, mix the melted coconut oil, chopped walnuts, cinnamon, sweetener, salt, and vanilla extract.
4. Pour the mixture over the apple wedges, tossing to coat evenly.
5. Bake for 25 minutes, or until the apples are tender and lightly caramelized.
6. Serve warm as a dessert or snack.

Nutritional Information (Per Serving):

- Total calories: 180
- Protein: 3g
- Fiber content: 5g
- Carbs: 20g
- Fats: 10g

No-Bake Lemon Cheesecake Cups

Time to Prepare: 15 minutes
Cook Time: 0 minutes
Servings: 4

List of Ingredients:

- 1 cup of cream cheese (softened)
- 1/2 cup of Greek yogurt (unsweetened)
- 1/4 cup of sugar-free sweetener (like erythritol or monk fruit)
- 1/4 cup of fresh lemon juice
- Zest of 1 lemon
- 1 teaspoon of vanilla extract
- 1/2 teaspoon of gelatin (optional, for firmer texture)
- Fresh berries (for topping, optional)

Instructions:

1. In a mixing bowl, combine softened cream cheese, Greek yogurt, sweetener, lemon juice, lemon zest, and vanilla extract. Mix until smooth and creamy.
2. If using, dissolve gelatin in 1 tablespoon of warm water and add to the mixture, stirring well.
3. Spoon the mixture into serving cups of and refrigerate for at least 2 hours to set.
4. Serve chilled, topped with fresh berries if desired.

Nutritional Information (Per Serving):

- Total calories: 150
- Protein: 6g
- Fiber content: 1g
- Carbs: 8g
- Fats: 12g

Dark Chocolate & Sea Salt Fat Bombs

Time to Prepare: 10 minutes
Cook Time: 0 minutes
Servings: 12

List of Ingredients:

- 1/2 cup of coconut oil (melted)
- 1/2 cup of unsweetened cocoa powder
- 1/4 cup of sugar-free sweetener (like erythritol or monk fruit)
- 1 teaspoon of vanilla extract
- 1/4 teaspoon of sea salt
- 1/4 cup of almond butter (or any nut butter)
- Sea salt flakes (for topping)

Instructions:

1. In a mixing bowl, combine melted coconut oil, cocoa powder, sweetener, vanilla extract, and sea salt. Stir until smooth.
2. Add the almond butter and mix until fully incorporated.
3. Pour the mixture into silicone molds or mini muffin cups, filling each about 3/4 full.
4. Sprinkle a pinch of sea salt flakes on top of each bomb.
5. Place the molds in the freezer for about 30 minutes or until solid.
6. Once set, remove from molds and store in an airtight container in the refrigerator or freezer.

Nutritional Information (Per Serving):

- Total calories: 120
- Protein: 1g
- Fiber content: 2g
- Carbs: 5g
- Fats: 12g

Raspberry Chia Seed Pudding

Time to Prepare: 10 minutes
Cook Time: 0 minutes
Servings: 4

List of Ingredients:

- 1 cup of unsweetened almond milk
- 1/2 cup of fresh raspberries (plus extra for topping)
- 1/4 cup of chia seeds
- 2 tablespoons sugar-free sweetener (like erythritol or monk fruit)
- 1 teaspoon of vanilla extract
- A pinch of salt

Instructions:

1. In a blender, combine almond milk, fresh raspberries, sweetener, vanilla extract, and salt. Blend until smooth.
2. In a mixing bowl, combine chia seeds with the raspberry mixture and stir well.
3. Let the mixture sit for about 5 minutes, then stir again to prevent clumping.
4. Cover the bowl and refrigerate for at least 2 hours or overnight until the pudding thickens.
5. Serve chilled, topped with additional fresh raspberries if desired.

Nutritional Information (Per Serving):

- Total calories: 100
- Protein: 3g
- Fiber content: 6g
- Carbs: 8g
- Fats: 5g

Coconut Almond Bliss Balls

Time to Prepare: 15 minutes
Cook Time: 0 minutes
Servings: 12

List of Ingredients:

- 1 cup of almond flour
- 1/2 cup of unsweetened shredded coconut
- 1/4 cup of almond butter
- 2 tablespoons sugar-free sweetener (like erythritol or monk fruit)
- 1 teaspoon of vanilla extract
- 1/4 teaspoon of salt
- 2 tablespoons coconut oil (melted)
- 1/4 cup of dark chocolate chips (sugar-free, optional)

Instructions:

1. In a mixing bowl, combine almond flour, shredded coconut, almond butter, sweetener, vanilla extract, salt, and melted coconut oil. Mix until a sticky dough forms.
2. If using, fold in dark chocolate chips.
3. Scoop out small portions of the mixture and roll into balls, about 1 inch in diameter.
4. Place the bliss balls on a parchment-lined tray and refrigerate for at least 30 minutes to firm up.
5. Store the bliss balls in an airtight container in the refrigerator for up to one week.

Nutritional Information (Per Serving):

- Total calories: 120
- Protein: 4g
- Fiber content: 3g
- Carbs: 7g
- Fats: 10g

Keto-Friendly Pumpkin Spice Muffins

Time to Prepare: 10 minutes
Cook Time: 25 minutes
Servings: 12

List of Ingredients:

- 1 cup of almond flour
- 1/2 cup of pumpkin puree (unsweetened)
- 1/4 cup of sugar-free sweetener (like erythritol or monk fruit)
- 2 large eggs
- 1/4 cup of coconut oil (melted)
- 1 teaspoon of vanilla extract
- 1 teaspoon of baking powder
- 1 teaspoon of pumpkin pie spice
- 1/2 teaspoon of cinnamon
- 1/4 teaspoon of salt

Instructions:

1. Preheat the oven to 350°F (175°C) and line a muffin tin with paper liners or grease it.
2. In a large mixing bowl, combine almond flour, pumpkin puree, sweetener, eggs, melted coconut oil, and vanilla extract. Mix until well mixed.
3. Add baking powder, pumpkin pie spice, cinnamon, and salt to the mixture. Stir until all ingredients are fully incorporated.
4. Divide the batter evenly among the muffin cups, filling each about 2/3 full.
5. Bake for 20-25 minutes, or until a toothpick inserted in the center comes out clean.
6. Allow the muffins to cool in the pan for 5 minutes before transferring to a wire rack to cool completely.

Nutritional Information (Per Serving):

- Total calories: 120
- Protein: 4g
- Fiber content: 2g
- Carbs: 6g
- Fats: 10g

Blueberry Crumble with Almond Topping

Time to Prepare: 15 minutes
Cook Time: 30 minutes
Servings: 8

List of Ingredients:

- 2 cups of fresh blueberries
- 1/4 cup of almond flour
- 1/4 cup of sugar-free sweetener (like erythritol or monk fruit)
- 1/4 cup of rolled oats (gluten-free if desired)
- 1/2 cup of sliced almonds
- 1/4 cup of coconut oil (melted)
- 1 teaspoon of vanilla extract
- 1 teaspoon of cinnamon
- 1/4 teaspoon of salt

Instructions:

1. Preheat the oven to 350°F (175°C) and grease a baking dish.
2. In a bowl, combine the fresh blueberries, 1 tablespoon of the sweetener, and half the cinnamon. Pour the blueberry mixture into the prepared baking dish.
3. In another bowl, mix together almond flour, oats, remaining sweetener, sliced almonds, melted coconut oil, remaining cinnamon, and salt until crumbly.
4. Sprinkle the almond topping evenly over the blueberries.
5. Bake for 25-30 minutes or until the topping is golden brown and the blueberries are bubbling.
6. Allow to cool slightly before serving.

Nutritional Information (Per Serving):

- Total calories: 150
- Protein: 4g
- Fiber content: 3g
- Carbs: 10g
- Fats: 11g

Vanilla Bean Coconut Ice Cream

Time to Prepare: 15 minutes
Cook Time: 4 hours (chill time)
Servings: 6

List of Ingredients:

- 1 can (13.5 oz) full-fat coconut milk
- 1/2 cup of unsweetened almond milk
- 1/4 cup of sugar-free sweetener (like erythritol or monk fruit)
- 1 tablespoon vanilla bean paste or 1 vanilla bean (scraped)
- 1 teaspoon of pure vanilla extract
- Pinch of salt

Instructions:

1. In a mixing bowl, combine the coconut milk, almond milk, sweetener, vanilla bean paste (or scraped vanilla bean), vanilla extract, and salt. Whisk until well mixed.
2. Pour the mixture into an ice cream maker and churn according to the manufacturer's instructions until it reaches a soft-serve consistency.
3. Transfer the ice cream to an airtight container and freeze for at least 4 hours, or until firm.
4. Before serving, let the ice cream sit at room temperature for a few minutes to soften slightly.

Nutritional Information (Per Serving):

- Total calories: 200
- Protein: 2g
- Fiber content: 1g
- Carbs: 8g
- Fats: 18g

Chocolate Avocado Pudding

Time to Prepare: 10 minutes
Cook Time: 0 minutes
Servings: 4

List of Ingredients:

- 2 ripe avocados
- 1/2 cup of unsweetened cocoa powder
- 1/3 cup of sugar-free sweetener (like erythritol or monk fruit)
- 1/2 cup of unsweetened almond milk
- 1 teaspoon of vanilla extract
- Pinch of salt

Instructions:

1. Cut the avocados in half, remove the pits, and scoop the flesh into a blender or food processor.
2. Add the cocoa powder, sweetener, almond milk, vanilla extract, and salt. Blend until smooth and creamy.
3. Taste and adjust sweetness if needed.
4. Transfer the pudding to serving bowls and refrigerate for at least 30 minutes before serving.

Nutritional Information (Per Serving):

- Total calories: 180
- Protein: 3g
- Fiber content: 7g
- Carbs: 13g
- Fats: 14g

Low-Carb Peanut Butter Bars

Time to Prepare: 15 minutes
Cook Time: 10 minutes
Servings: 12

List of Ingredients:

- 1 cup of natural peanut butter (sugar-free)
- 1/4 cup of sugar-free sweetener (like erythritol or monk fruit)
- 1/2 cup of unsweetened almond flour
- 1/4 cup of unsweetened cocoa powder
- 1 teaspoon of vanilla extract
- 1/4 teaspoon of salt
- 2 tablespoons coconut oil (melted)

Instructions:

1. Preheat the oven to 350°F (175°C) and line an 8x8 inch baking dish with parchment paper.
2. In a mixing bowl, combine peanut butter, sweetener, almond flour, cocoa powder, vanilla extract, salt, and melted coconut oil. Mix until well mixed.
3. Spread the mixture evenly in the prepared baking dish, pressing down firmly.
4. Bake for 10 minutes, then remove from the oven and let cool completely.
5. Once cooled, cut into bars and store in the refrigerator.

Nutritional Information (Per Serving):

- Total calories: 150
- Protein: 6g
- Fiber content: 2g
- Carbs: 5g
- Fats: 12g

Strawberry Coconut Popsicles

Time to Prepare: 10 minutes
Cook Time: 0 minutes
Servings: 6

List of Ingredients:

- 2 cups of fresh strawberries, hulled and chopped
- 1 cup of coconut milk (full-fat, unsweetened)
- 2 tablespoons sugar-free sweetener (like erythritol or monk fruit)
- 1 teaspoon of vanilla extract

Instructions:

1. In a blender, combine the strawberries, coconut milk, sweetener, and vanilla extract. Blend until smooth.
2. Pour the mixture into popsicle molds, leaving a little space at the top for expansion.
3. Insert sticks and freeze for at least 4-6 hours or until solid.
4. To release the popsicles, run warm water over the outside of the molds for a few seconds.

Nutritional Information (Per Serving):

- Total calories: 70
- Protein: 1g
- Fiber content: 2g
- Carbs: 6g
- Fats: 5g

Mini Berry Cheesecakes

Time to Prepare: 15 minutes
Cook Time: 20 minutes
Servings: 12

List of Ingredients:

- 1 cup of almond flour
- 1/4 cup of melted butter
- 2 tablespoons sugar-free sweetener (like erythritol or monk fruit)
- 8 oz cream cheese, softened
- 1/4 cup of sour cream
- 1/4 cup of sugar-free sweetener
- 1 teaspoon of vanilla extract
- 1 cup of mixed berries (strawberries, blueberries, raspberries)

Instructions:

1. Preheat the oven to 350°F (175°C). Line a muffin tin with cupcake liners.
2. In a mixing bowl, combine the almond flour, melted butter, and 2 tablespoons of sweetener. Press the mixture into the bottom of each cupcake liner to form the crust.
3. In another bowl, beat the cream cheese until smooth. Add the sour cream, 1/4 cup of sweetener, and vanilla extract, mixing until well mixed.
4. Divide the cream cheese mixture evenly among the crusts in the muffin tin.
5. Top each cheesecake with mixed berries.
6. Bake for 20 minutes, then remove from the oven and let cool. Refrigerate for at least 2 hours before serving.

Nutritional Information (Per Serving):

- Total calories: 120
- Protein: 4g
- Fiber content: 2g
- Carbs: 5g
- Fats: 10g

Baked Pears with Cinnamon and Almonds

Time to Prepare: 10 minutes
Cook Time: 25 minutes
Servings: 4

List of Ingredients:

- 4 medium pears, halved and cored
- 1/4 cup of sliced almonds
- 2 tablespoons butter, melted
- 1 teaspoon of cinnamon
- 2 tablespoons sugar-free sweetener (like erythritol or monk fruit)
- 1 tablespoon lemon juice

Instructions:

1. Preheat the oven to 350°F (175°C).
2. Place the halved pears in a baking dish, cut side up.
3. In a small bowl, mix together the melted butter, cinnamon, sweetener, and lemon juice.
4. Brush the mixture over the pears evenly.
5. Sprinkle the sliced almonds on top of the pears.
6. Bake in the preheated oven for 25 minutes, or until the pears are tender and lightly browned.
7. Serve warm, optionally drizzled with additional melted butter or sweetener if desired.

Nutritional Information (Per Serving):

- Total calories: 150
- Protein: 2g
- Fiber content: 4g
- Carbs: 16g
- Fats: 8g

Keto-Friendly Chocolate Chip Blondies

Time to Prepare: 10 minutes
Cook Time: 25 minutes
Servings: 12

List of Ingredients:

- 1 cup of almond flour
- 1/2 cup of unsalted butter, melted
- 1/2 cup of sugar-free sweetener (like erythritol or monk fruit)
- 2 large eggs
- 1 teaspoon of vanilla extract
- 1/2 teaspoon of baking powder
- 1/4 teaspoon of salt
- 1/2 cup of sugar-free chocolate chips

Instructions:

1. Preheat the oven to 350°F (175°C). Line an 8x8 inch baking pan with parchment paper.
2. In a mixing bowl, combine the melted butter and sweetener until well blended.
3. Add the eggs and vanilla extract, mixing until smooth.
4. In a separate bowl, whisk together the almond flour, baking powder, and salt.
5. Gradually add the dry ingredients to the wet mixture, stirring until fully incorporated.
6. Fold in the sugar-free chocolate chips.
7. Pour the batter into the prepared baking pan and spread it evenly.
8. Bake for 25 minutes or until golden brown and a toothpick comes out clean.
9. Let cool before cutting into squares and serving.

Nutritional Information (Per Serving):

- Total calories: 150
- Protein: 3g
- Fiber content: 2g
- Carbs: 4g
- Fats: 14g

Matcha Coconut Fudge

Time to Prepare: 15 minutes
Cook Time: 0 minutes
Servings: 12

List of Ingredients:

- 1 cup of coconut butter, melted
- 1/2 cup of unsweetened shredded coconut
- 1/4 cup of coconut oil, melted
- 1/4 cup of sugar-free sweetener (like erythritol or monk fruit)
- 2 tablespoons matcha powder
- 1 teaspoon of vanilla extract
- Pinch of salt

Instructions:

1. In a mixing bowl, combine melted coconut butter, melted coconut oil, and sugar-free sweetener until smooth.
2. Add matcha powder, vanilla extract, and salt, mixing until well incorporated.
3. Fold in the shredded coconut.
4. Pour the mixture into a lined 8x8 inch baking dish, spreading it evenly.
5. Refrigerate for at least 2 hours or until firm.
6. Once set, cut into squares and serve chilled or at room temperature.

Nutritional Information (Per Serving):

- Total calories: 120
- Protein: 1g
- Fiber content: 2g
- Carbs: 3g
- Fats: 12g

CHAPTER 7: BEVERAGES & SMOOTHIES

Green Detox Smoothie with Spinach & Pineapple

Time to Prepare: 10 minutes
Cook Time: 0 minutes
Servings: 2

List of Ingredients:

- 2 cups of fresh spinach
- 1 cup of frozen pineapple chunks
- 1 medium avocado
- 1 cup of unsweetened almond milk
- 1 tablespoon chia seeds
- 1 tablespoon fresh lemon juice
- 1 tablespoon fresh ginger, grated
- Ice cubes (optional)

Instructions:

1. In a blender, combine spinach, frozen pineapple, avocado, almond milk, chia seeds, lemon juice, and ginger.
2. Blend on high until smooth and creamy.
3. Add ice cubes if desired, and blend again until the desired consistency is reached.
4. Pour into glasses and serve immediately.

Nutritional Information (Per Serving):

- Total calories: 180
- Protein: 4g
- Fiber content: 8g
- Carbs: 20g
- Fats: 9g

Golden Turmeric Latte

Time to Prepare: 5 minutes
Cook Time: 5 minutes
Servings: 2

List of Ingredients:

- 2 cups of unsweetened almond milk
- 1 teaspoon of ground turmeric
- 1/2 teaspoon of ground cinnamon
- 1/4 teaspoon of ground ginger
- 1 tablespoon coconut oil
- 1 tablespoon maple syrup (optional, for sweetness)
- Pinch of black pepper
- 1/2 teaspoon of vanilla extract

Instructions:

1. In a small saucepan, combine almond milk, turmeric, cinnamon, ginger, and black pepper.
2. Heat over medium heat, stirring until warm but not boiling.
3. Remove from heat and whisk in coconut oil, maple syrup (if using), and vanilla extract until well mixed.
4. Pour into mugs and serve immediately.

Nutritional Information (Per Serving):

- Total calories: 130
- Protein: 2g
- Fiber content: 1g
- Carbs: 6g
- Fats: 12g

Cucumber Mint Infused Water

Time to Prepare: 10 minutes
Cook Time: 0 minutes
Servings: 4

List of Ingredients:

- 1 large cucumber, thinly sliced
- 1 cup of fresh mint leaves
- 8 cups of water
- Ice cubes (optional)

Instructions:

1. In a large pitcher, add the sliced cucumber and fresh mint leaves.
2. Pour in the water and stir gently to combine.
3. Refrigerate for at least 1 hour to allow the flavors to infuse.
4. Serve over ice if desired.

Nutritional Information (Per Serving):

- Total calories: 0
- Protein: 0g
- Fiber content: 0g
- Carbs: 0g
- Fats: 0g

Almond Butter & Banana Protein Shake

Time to Prepare: 5 minutes
Cook Time: 0 minutes
Servings: 1

List of Ingredients:

- 1 ripe banana
- 1 tablespoon almond butter
- 1 cup of unsweetened almond milk
- 1 scoop vanilla protein powder (low-carb)
- 1/2 teaspoon of cinnamon
- Ice cubes (optional)

Instructions:

1. In a blender, combine the banana, almond butter, almond milk, protein powder, and cinnamon.
2. Blend until smooth and creamy.
3. Add ice cubes if desired and blend again until well mixed.
4. Pour into a glass and enjoy immediately.

Nutritional Information (Per Serving):

- Total calories: 350
- Protein: 20g
- Fiber content: 5g
- Carbs: 30g
- Fats: 15g

Keto Iced Matcha Latte

Time to Prepare: 5 minutes
Cook Time: 0 minutes
Servings: 1

List of Ingredients:

- 1 teaspoon of matcha green tea powder
- 1 cup of unsweetened almond milk
- 1 tablespoon MCT oil or coconut oil
- 1-2 tablespoons erythritol or monk fruit sweetener (to taste)
- Ice cubes
- Optional: whipped coconut cream for topping

Instructions:

1. In a small bowl, whisk the matcha powder with a splash of hot water until smooth and no lumps remain.
2. In a glass, combine the matcha mixture, almond milk, MCT oil, and sweetener. Stir well to combine.
3. Fill the glass with ice cubes and stir again until chilled.
4. Top with whipped coconut cream if desired and serve immediately.

Nutritional Information (Per Serving):

- Total calories: 200
- Protein: 3g
- Fiber content: 1g
- Carbs: 5g
- Fats: 18g

Berry-Mint Lemonade

Time to Prepare: 10 minutes
Cook Time: 0 minutes
Servings: 4

List of Ingredients:

- 1 cup of fresh berries (strawberries, blueberries, or raspberries)
- 1/4 cup of fresh lemon juice
- 2 cups of water
- 2 tablespoons erythritol or monk fruit sweetener (adjust to taste)
- Fresh mint leaves (for garnish)
- Ice cubes

Instructions:

1. In a blender, combine the fresh berries and water. Blend until smooth.
2. Strain the mixture through a fine mesh sieve into a pitcher to remove seeds and pulp.
3. Add the fresh lemon juice and sweetener to the berry liquid. Stir well until the sweetener is dissolved.
4. Fill glasses with ice cubes and pour the berry-mint lemonade over the ice.
5. Garnish with fresh mint leaves and additional berries if desired. Serve immediately.

Nutritional Information (Per Serving):

- Total calories: 25
- Protein: 0g
- Fiber content: 1g
- Carbs: 6g
- Fats: 0g

Avocado Green Smoothie

Time to Prepare: 10 minutes
Cook Time: 0 minutes
Servings: 2

List of Ingredients:

- 1 ripe avocado
- 1 cup of spinach
- 1/2 cucumber, peeled and chopped
- 1/2 cup of unsweetened almond milk
- 1/2 cup of water
- 1 tablespoon chia seeds
- 1 tablespoon lemon juice
- 1/2 teaspoon of stevia or erythritol (optional, to taste)
- Ice cubes

Instructions:

1. In a blender, combine the avocado, spinach, cucumber, almond milk, water, chia seeds, lemon juice, and sweetener (if using).
2. Blend on high until smooth and creamy.
3. Adjust the consistency with more water if desired.
4. Add ice cubes and blend again until frosty.
5. Pour into glasses and serve immediately.

Nutritional Information (Per Serving):

- Total calories: 170
- Protein: 4g
- Fiber content: 9g
- Carbs: 13g
- Fats: 12g

Anti-Inflammatory Ginger Tea

Time to Prepare: 5 minutes
Cook Time: 10 minutes
Servings: 2

List of Ingredients:

- 2 cups of water
- 2-inch piece of fresh ginger, sliced
- 1 tablespoon lemon juice
- 1 tablespoon honey or stevia (optional, to taste)
- Pinch of cayenne pepper (optional)
- Fresh mint leaves (for garnish)

Instructions:

1. In a saucepan, bring the water to a boil.
2. Add the sliced ginger and reduce the heat to a simmer.
3. Allow the ginger to simmer for about 10 minutes to infuse the flavors.
4. Remove from heat and strain the tea into cups.
5. Stir in the lemon juice and sweetener (if using).
6. Garnish with fresh mint leaves and a pinch of cayenne pepper if desired.
7. Serve warm and enjoy.

Nutritional Information (Per Serving):

- Total calories: 30
- Protein: 0g
- Fiber content: 0g
- Carbs: 8g
- Fats: 0g

Strawberry & Basil Infused Sparkling Water

Time to Prepare: 5 minutes
Cook Time: 0 minutes
Servings: 4

List of Ingredients:

- 4 cups of sparkling water
- 1 cup of fresh strawberries, hulled and sliced
- 1/4 cup of fresh basil leaves
- Ice cubes (optional)
- Lemon slices (for garnish, optional)

Instructions:

1. In a pitcher, combine the sliced strawberries and fresh basil leaves.
2. Muddle the strawberries and basil gently to release their flavors.
3. Fill glasses with ice cubes (if using) and pour in the sparkling water.
4. Add the strawberry and basil mixture to the sparkling water and stir gently.
5. Garnish with lemon slices if desired.
6. Serve immediately and enjoy the refreshing drink.

Nutritional Information (Per Serving):

- Total calories: 10
- Protein: 0g
- Fiber content: 0g
- Carbs: 2g
- Fats: 0g

Spiced Chai Coconut Milk Latte

Time to Prepare: 5 minutes
Cook Time: 10 minutes
Servings: 2

List of Ingredients:

- 2 cups of unsweetened coconut milk
- 2 chai tea bags
- 1 teaspoon of ground cinnamon
- 1/2 teaspoon of ground ginger
- 1/4 teaspoon of ground cardamom
- 1 tablespoon monk fruit sweetener (or to taste)
- 1/2 teaspoon of vanilla extract (optional)

Instructions:

1. In a saucepan, heat the coconut milk over medium heat until warm, but not boiling.
2. Add the chai tea bags to the warm coconut milk and steep for 5-7 minutes.
3. Remove the tea bags and stir in the cinnamon, ginger, cardamom, monk fruit sweetener, and vanilla extract (if using).
4. Whisk the mixture until frothy, or use a milk frother for a creamier texture.
5. Divide the latte between two mugs and serve hot.

Nutritional Information (Per Serving):

- Total calories: 90
- Protein: 1g
- Fiber content: 2g
- Carbs: 5g
- Fats: 8g

Low-Carb Chocolate Peanut Butter Smoothie

Time to Prepare: 5 minutes
Cook Time: 0 minutes
Servings: 1

List of Ingredients:

- 1 cup of unsweetened almond milk
- 1 tablespoon natural peanut butter
- 1 tablespoon unsweetened cocoa powder
- 1 scoop low-carb protein powder (chocolate or vanilla)
- 1 tablespoon monk fruit sweetener (or to taste)
- Ice cubes (optional)

Instructions:

1. In a blender, combine the almond milk, peanut butter, cocoa powder, protein powder, and monk fruit sweetener.
2. Blend on high until smooth and creamy.
3. Add ice cubes if desired and blend again until the desired consistency is reached.
4. Pour into a glass and enjoy immediately.

Nutritional Information:

- Total calories: 300
- Protein: 25g
- Fiber content: 6g
- Carbs: 9g
- Fats: 20g

Citrus & Mint Green Tea Cooler

Time to Prepare: 10 minutes
Cook Time: 5 minutes
Servings: 2

List of Ingredients:

- 2 cups of water
- 2 green tea bags
- 1 tablespoon fresh mint leaves
- Juice of 1 lemon
- Juice of 1 lime
- 1 tablespoon monk fruit sweetener (or to taste)
- Lemon and lime slices for garnish
- Fresh mint sprigs for garnish
- Ice cubes

Instructions:

1. Bring the water to a boil in a small saucepan.
2. Remove from heat and add the green tea bags and mint leaves. Steep for 5 minutes.
3. Remove the tea bags and mint leaves, then stir in the lemon juice, lime juice, and monk fruit sweetener until dissolved.
4. Let the tea cool to room temperature, then refrigerate until chilled.
5. Serve over ice, garnished with lemon and lime slices and fresh mint sprigs.

Nutritional Information:

- Total calories: 20
- Protein: 0g
- Fiber content: 0g
- Carbs: 5g
- Fats: 0g

Keto Pumpkin Spice Coffee

Time to Prepare: 5 minutes
Cook Time: 5 minutes
Servings: 1

List of Ingredients:

- 1 cup of brewed coffee
- 2 tablespoons canned pumpkin puree
- 1 tablespoon unsweetened cocoa powder
- 1 tablespoon almond butter (or coconut cream)
- 1/2 teaspoon of pumpkin pie spice
- 1 tablespoon monk fruit sweetener (or to taste)
- 1/4 cup of unsweetened almond milk (or coconut milk)
- Whipped cream (optional, sugar-free)

Instructions:

1. Brew your favorite coffee.
2. In a blender, combine the hot coffee, pumpkin puree, cocoa powder, almond butter, pumpkin pie spice, monk fruit sweetener, and almond milk.
3. Blend until smooth and frothy.
4. Pour into a mug and top with whipped cream if desired.

Nutritional Information:

- Total calories: 250
- Protein: 5g
- Fiber content: 5g
- Carbs: 10g
- Fats: 20g

Blueberry-Cucumber Hydration Smoothie

Time to Prepare: 10 minutes
Cook Time: 0 minutes
Servings: 2

List of Ingredients:

- 1 cup of fresh blueberries
- 1 medium cucumber, peeled and chopped
- 1 cup of unsweetened almond milk (or coconut milk)
- 1 tablespoon chia seeds
- 1 tablespoon monk fruit sweetener (optional)
- Juice of 1/2 lemon
- Ice cubes (optional)

Instructions:

1. In a blender, combine the blueberries, cucumber, almond milk, chia seeds, monk fruit sweetener, and lemon juice.
2. Blend until smooth.
3. If desired, add ice cubes and blend again for a chilled smoothie.
4. Pour into glasses and serve immediately.

Nutritional Information:

- Total calories: 120
- Protein: 3g
- Fiber content: 6g
- Carbs: 20g
- Fats: 4g

Ginger & Lemon Detox Water

Time to Prepare: 10 minutes
Cook Time: 0 minutes
Servings: 4

List of Ingredients:

- 4 cups of filtered water
- 1-inch piece of fresh ginger, sliced
- 1 lemon, sliced
- Fresh mint leaves (optional)

Instructions:

1. In a large pitcher, combine the filtered water, sliced ginger, and lemon.
2. If desired, add a handful of fresh mint leaves for extra flavor.
3. Stir well and let the mixture sit in the refrigerator for at least 1-2 hours to allow the flavors to infuse.
4. Serve chilled, adding ice if desired.

Nutritional Information:

- Total calories: 10
- Protein: 0g
- Fiber content: 0g
- Carbs: 3g
- Fats: 0g

Almond Milk Hot Chocolate

Time to Prepare: 5 minutes
Cook Time: 5 minutes
Servings: 2

List of Ingredients:

- 2 cups of unsweetened almond milk
- 2 tablespoons unsweetened cocoa powder
- 2 tablespoons erythritol or preferred sweetener
- 1 teaspoon of vanilla extract
- A pinch of sea salt
- Optional: whipped coconut cream for topping

Instructions:

1. In a small saucepan, heat the almond milk over medium heat until warm but not boiling.
2. Whisk in the cocoa powder, erythritol, vanilla extract, and a pinch of sea salt until smooth and well mixed.
3. Continue to heat for another minute, stirring frequently.
4. Remove from heat and pour into two mugs.
5. If desired, top with whipped coconut cream before serving.

Nutritional Information:

- Total calories: 60
- Protein: 2g
- Fiber content: 4g
- Carbs: 10g
- Fats: 2g

Mango-Turmeric Smoothie

Time to Prepare: 5 minutes
Cook Time: 0 minutes
Servings: 2

List of Ingredients:

- 1 cup of frozen mango chunks
- 1 cup of unsweetened almond milk
- 1 teaspoon of ground turmeric
- 1 tablespoon chia seeds
- 1 tablespoon lemon juice
- A pinch of black pepper (to enhance turmeric absorption)
- Optional: ice cubes for a thicker consistency

Instructions:

1. In a blender, combine the frozen mango chunks, almond milk, turmeric, chia seeds, lemon juice, and black pepper.
2. Blend until smooth and creamy.
3. If you prefer a thicker smoothie, add a few ice cubes and blend again until desired consistency is reached.
4. Pour into glasses and serve immediately.

Nutritional Information:

- Total calories: 160
- Protein: 4g
- Fiber content: 6g
- Carbs: 28g
- Fats: 4g

WALTER RIVERS

30-DAY MEAL PLAN

Day	Breakfast	Lunch	Snacks	Dinner
1	Avocado & Spinach Breakfast Smoothie	Grilled Chicken & Avocado Salad	Cucumber & Smoked Salmon Roll-Ups	Garlic Butter Baked Salmon with Asparagus
2	Keto Chia Seed Pudding with Fresh Berries	Creamy Broccoli & Cheddar Soup	Keto-Friendly Cheese Crisps	Zesty Lemon-Herb Chicken Thighs
3	Egg White & Veggie Frittata	Keto Taco Salad with Ground Turkey	Zucchini Chips with Herb Dip	Beef & Veggie Stir-Fry with Coconut Aminos
4	Almond Flour Pancakes with Sugar-Free Syrup	Spinach & Feta Stuffed Portobello Mushrooms	Spicy Almond Butter Energy Balls	Sheet Pan Shrimp Fajitas
5	Smoked Salmon & Avocado Breakfast Bowl	Asian-Inspired Shrimp & Cabbage Stir-Fry	Roasted Garlic & Parmesan Kale Chips	Spaghetti Squash with Pesto & Grilled Chicken
6	Coconut Yogurt Parfait with Chopped Nuts	Cauliflower Fried "Rice" with Beef	Stuffed Mini Bell Peppers with Cream Cheese	Cauliflower Crust Margherita Pizza
7	Cauliflower Hash Browns with Poached Eggs	Lemon-Dill Salmon Lettuce Wraps	Crispy Avocado Fries	Keto-Friendly Lasagna with Zucchini Noodles
8	Spicy Egg Muffins with Bell Peppers	Greek Chicken Salad with Cucumber & Olives	Mini Caprese Skewers with Balsamic Glaze	Seared Ahi Tuna with Ginger-Cucumber Slaw
9	Zucchini Noodles Breakfast Bowl with Pesto	Zucchini Noodle Alfredo with Grilled Chicken	Cauliflower Hummus with Veggie Sticks	Rosemary-Garlic Pork Tenderloin
10	Cinnamon Flaxseed Porridge	Low-Carb BLT Wraps	Deviled Eggs with Smoked Paprika	Miso Cod with Bok Choy
11	Low-Carb Breakfast Burrito with Turkey Sausage	Garlic & Herb Roasted Veggie Bowl	Baked Buffalo Cauliflower Bites	Chicken & Mushroom Creamy Cauliflower Rice
12	Keto Avocado Toast on Almond Flour Bread	Buffalo Chicken Stuffed Avocados	Almond Butter and Celery Sticks	Greek-Inspired Lamb Burgers with Tzatziki Sauce
13	Berry & Coconut Smoothie Bowl	Curried Cauliflower Soup with Coconut Milk	Keto-Friendly Trail Mix with Nuts & Seeds	Slow-Cooked Beef Stew with Root Vegetables
14	Sautéed Mushrooms & Spinach Omelet	Italian Meatball Zoodle Soup	Garlic & Herb Roasted Pumpkin Seeds	Stuffed Bell Peppers with Ground Turkey & Veggies
15	Bacon-Wrapped Asparagus with Soft-Boiled Eggs	Cajun Shrimp & Avocado Salad	Mini Cucumber Sandwiches with Turkey & Avocado	Roasted Lemon-Garlic Brussels Sprouts & Sausage

16	Matcha Coconut Latte	Grilled Chicken & Avocado Salad	Frozen Coconut Berry Bites	Thai-Inspired Coconut Curry Chicken
17	Blueberry-Almond Protein Smoothie	Creamy Broccoli & Cheddar Soup	Cucumber & Smoked Salmon Roll-Ups	Herbed Butter Roasted Whole Chicken
18	Avocado & Spinach Breakfast Smoothie	Keto Taco Salad with Ground Turkey	Keto-Friendly Cheese Crisps	Garlic Butter Baked Salmon with Asparagus
19	Keto Chia Seed Pudding with Fresh Berries	Spinach & Feta Stuffed Portobello Mushrooms	Zucchini Chips with Herb Dip	Zesty Lemon-Herb Chicken Thighs
20	Egg White & Veggie Frittata	Asian-Inspired Shrimp & Cabbage Stir-Fry	Spicy Almond Butter Energy Balls	Beef & Veggie Stir-Fry with Coconut Aminos
21	Almond Flour Pancakes with Sugar-Free Syrup	Cauliflower Fried "Rice" with Beef	Roasted Garlic & Parmesan Kale Chips	Sheet Pan Shrimp Fajitas
22	Smoked Salmon & Avocado Breakfast Bowl	Lemon-Dill Salmon Lettuce Wraps	Stuffed Mini Bell Peppers with Cream Cheese	Spaghetti Squash with Pesto & Grilled Chicken
23	Coconut Yogurt Parfait with Chopped Nuts	Greek Chicken Salad with Cucumber & Olives	Crispy Avocado Fries	Cauliflower Crust Margherita Pizza
24	Cauliflower Hash Browns with Poached Eggs	Zucchini Noodle Alfredo with Grilled Chicken	Mini Caprese Skewers with Balsamic Glaze	Keto-Friendly Lasagna with Zucchini Noodles
25	Spicy Egg Muffins with Bell Peppers	Zucchini Noodle Alfredo with Grilled Chicken	Cauliflower Hummus with Veggie Sticks	Rosemary-Garlic Pork Tenderloin
26	Zucchini Noodles Breakfast Bowl with Pesto	Italian Meatball Zoodle Soup	Garlic & Herb Roasted Pumpkin Seeds	Miso Cod with Bok Choy
27	Cinnamon Flaxseed Porridge	Buffalo Chicken Stuffed Avocados	Deviled Eggs with Smoked Paprika	Chicken & Mushroom Creamy Cauliflower Rice
28	Low-Carb Breakfast Burrito with Turkey Sausage	Curried Cauliflower Soup with Coconut Milk	Almond Butter and Celery Sticks	Greek-Inspired Lamb Burgers with Tzatziki Sauce
29	Keto Avocado Toast on Almond Flour Bread	Slow-Cooked Beef Stew with Root Vegetables	Keto-Friendly Trail Mix with Nuts & Seeds	Roasted Lemon-Garlic Brussels Sprouts & Sausage
30	Berry & Coconut Smoothie Bowl	Balsamic Chicken & Roasted Veggie Sheet Pan Meal	Mini Cucumber Sandwiches with Turkey & Avocado	Thai-Inspired Coconut Curry Chicken

MEASUREMENT CONVERSION TABLE

Measurement	Imperial (US)	Metric
Volume		
1 teaspoon	1 tsp	5 milliliters
1 tablespoon	1 tbsp	15 milliliters
1 fluid ounce	1 fl oz	30 milliliters
1 cup	1 cup	240 milliliters
1 pint	1 pt	473 milliliters
1 quart	1 qt	0.95 liters
1 gallon	1 gal	3.8 liters
Weight		
1 ounce	1 oz	28 grams
1 pound	1 lb	454 grams
Temperature		
32°F	32°F	0°C
212°F	212°F	100°C
Other		
1 stick of butter	1 stick	113 grams

CONCLUSION

As we finish our exploration of the Galveston Diet, it's important to keep in mind that living healthily involves more than just what you eat. It's also about developing a mindset that prioritizes wellness, balance, and sustainability. This cookbook offers recipes and meal plans that help you enjoy tasty and healthy options that match your health goals.

Using low-carb, nutrient-rich ingredients in your meals can help you lose weight, boost your energy, and enhance your overall health. Keep in mind that success comes from having a mix and balance—feel free to combine recipes or change them to suit your taste. Try out new tastes, play around with various ingredients, and enjoy the journey of making meals that feed both your body and spirit.

This cookbook is here to help you and inspire you to make the Galveston Diet a lasting part of your life. By staying dedicated and being creative, you can reach your health goals and still enjoy the tasty foods you love. Here's to your path to becoming a healthier and happier version of yourself!

RECIPES INDEX

Almond Butter & Banana Protein Shake 100

Almond Butter and Celery Sticks 34

Almond Flour Pancakes with Sugar-Free Syrup 9

Almond Flour Shortbread Cookies 83

Almond Milk Hot Chocolate 106

Anti-Inflammatory Ginger Tea 102

Asian-Inspired Shrimp & Cabbage Stir-Fry 44

Avocado & Spinach Breakfast Smoothie 6

Avocado Green Smoothie 102

Bacon-Wrapped Asparagus with Soft-Boiled Eggs 20

Baked Buffalo Cauliflower Bites 33

Baked Cinnamon Apples with Walnuts 84

Baked Pears with Cinnamon and Almonds 96

Baked Zucchini Fries 80

Balsamic Chicken & Roasted Veggie Sheet Pan Meal 53

Balsamic Glazed Brussels Sprouts with Pecans 74

Beef & Veggie Stir-Fry with Coconut Aminos 58

Berry & Coconut Smoothie Bowl 18

Berry-Mint Lemonade 101

Blueberry Crumble with Almond Topping 90

Blueberry-Almond Protein Smoothie 22

Blueberry-Cucumber Hydration Smoothie 105

Buttery Cabbage Steaks 77

Cajun Shrimp & Avocado Salad 55

Cauliflower "Mac & Cheese" 78

Cauliflower Crust Margherita Pizza 61

Cauliflower Fried "Rice" with Beef 45

Cauliflower Hash Browns with Poached Eggs 12

Cauliflower Hummus with Veggie Sticks 31

Cheesy Cauliflower Mash 76

Chicken & Mushroom Creamy Cauliflower Rice 66

Chocolate Avocado Pudding 92

Cinnamon Flaxseed Porridge 15

Citrus & Mint Green Tea Cooler 104

Coconut Almond Bliss Balls 88

Coconut Yogurt Parfait with Chopped Nuts 11

Creamy Avocado & Cucumber Salad 79

Creamy Broccoli & Cheddar Soup 41

Crispy Avocado Fries 29

Crispy Baked Kale with Sea Salt 76

Cucumber & Smoked Salmon Roll-Ups 23

Cucumber Mint Infused Water 100

Curried Cauliflower Soup with Coconut Milk 51

Dark Chocolate & Sea Salt Fat Bombs 86

Deviled Eggs with Smoked Paprika 32

Egg White & Veggie Frittata 8

Frozen Coconut Berry Bites 39

Garlic & Herb Roasted Pumpkin Seeds 36

Garlic & Herb Roasted Veggie Bowl 50

Garlic Butter Baked Salmon with Asparagus 56

Garlic Lemon Green Beans 80

Garlic Parmesan Roasted Broccoli 73

Ginger & Lemon Detox Water 106

Golden Turmeric Latte 99

Greek Chicken Salad with Cucumber & Olives 47

Greek-Inspired Lamb Burgers with Tzatziki Sauce 67

Green Detox Smoothie with Spinach & Pineapple 99

Grilled Asparagus with Lemon Zest 75

Grilled Chicken & Avocado Salad with Lime Vinaigrette 40

Herbed Butter Roasted Whole Chicken 72

Italian Meatball Zoodle Soup 52

Keto Avocado Toast on Almond Flour Bread 17

Keto Chia Seed Pudding with Fresh Berries 7

THE GALVESTON DIET COOKBOOK FOR BEGINNERS 2025

Keto Chocolate Mousse with Coconut Cream 82

Keto Iced Matcha Latte 101

Keto Pumpkin Spice Coffee 105

Keto Taco Salad with Ground Turkey 42

Keto-Friendly Cheese Crisps 24

Keto-Friendly Chocolate Chip Blondies 97

Keto-Friendly Lasagna with Zucchini Noodles 62

Keto-Friendly Pumpkin Spice Muffins 89

Keto-Friendly Trail Mix with Nuts & Seeds 35

Lemon-Dill Salmon Lettuce Wraps 46

Low-Carb BLT Wraps 49

Low-Carb Breakfast Burrito with Turkey Sausage 16

Low-Carb Chocolate Peanut Butter Smoothie 104

Low-Carb Peanut Butter Bars 93

Mango-Turmeric Smoothie 107

Matcha Coconut Fudge 98

Matcha Coconut Latte 21

Mini Berry Cheesecakes 95

Mini Caprese Skewers with Balsamic Glaze 30

Mini Cucumber Sandwiches with Turkey & Avocado 37

Miso Cod with Bok Choy 65

No-Bake Lemon Cheesecake Cups 85

Raspberry Chia Seed Pudding 87

Roasted Garlic & Parmesan Kale Chips 27

Roasted Lemon-Garlic Brussels Sprouts & Sausage 70

Roasted Radishes with Rosemary 78

Roasted Rainbow Carrots with Thyme 75

Rosemary-Garlic Pork Tenderloin 64

Sautéed Mushrooms & Spinach Omelet 19

Sautéed Mushrooms with Fresh Herbs 79

Seared Ahi Tuna with Ginger-Cucumber Slaw 63

Sheet Pan Shrimp Fajitas 59

Slow-Cooked Beef Stew with Root Vegetables 68

Smoked Salmon & Avocado Breakfast Bowl 10

Spaghetti Squash with Pesto & Grilled Chicken 60

Spiced Chai Coconut Milk Latte 103

Spicy Almond Butter Energy Balls 26

Spicy Cauliflower Rice Pilaf 73

Spicy Egg Muffins with Bell Peppers 13

Spicy Sautéed Spinach with Garlic 77

Spicy Tuna Salad Lettuce Wraps 38

Spinach & Feta Stuffed Portobello Mushrooms 43

Strawberry & Basil Infused Sparkling Water 103

Strawberry Coconut Popsicles 94

Stuffed Bell Peppers with Ground Turkey & Veggies 69

Stuffed Mini Bell Peppers with Cream Cheese 28

Sweet & Spicy Roasted Butternut Squash 81

Thai-Inspired Coconut Curry Chicken 71

Tuna & Egg Salad on Butter Lettuce 54

Vanilla Bean Coconut Ice Cream 91

Zesty Lemon-Herb Chicken Thighs 57

Zoodles with Sun-Dried Tomato & Olive Tapenade 74

Zucchini Chips with Herb Dip 25

Zucchini Noodle Alfredo with Grilled Chicken 48

Zucchini Noodles Breakfast Bowl with Pesto 14

Printed in Dunstable, United Kingdom